THE
franciscan
CHAR
IN THE CHU...

ANSELM W. ROMB, O. F. M. CONV.

ST. ANTHONY GUILD PRESS
PATERSON, NEW JERSEY

This book is dedicated
to the
dear memory of my father
Joseph Jerome Romb
and the
living presence of my mother
Aurelia Wanda Romb
who possess
the Franciscan charism
without trying
to define it

FOREWORD

I owe a special debt of gratitude to the work of Fr. Raphael Huber, O. F. M. Conv., concerning early Franciscan history and the sources for the life of St. Francis as they are found in his scholarly book *A Documented History of the Franciscan Order.* Similarly, research was infinitely easier for having had at hand the compact book by Fr. James Meyer, O. F. M., *The Words of St. Francis.* To all my confreres of St. Bonaventure Province I express my thanks for helping me evolve my concepts in dialogue as I alternated between the roles of Savonarola and Diogenes for the last eighteen years. Finally, I am grateful to Fr. John Chrysostom Simms, O. F. M. Conv., for having read and commented on the manuscript.

This book is addressed not only to members of the First Order, but also to the Second Order of Clares and the Third Order, both "regular" and "secular." Perhaps the diocesan clergy, those who are struggling to define their own charism, and other observers of the ecclesiastical scene will profit from this effort. In any case this book must be judged as it is presented, namely, as one man's opinion.

Fr. Anselm W. Romb, O. F. M. Conv.
Loyola University
Chicago, Illinois

CONTENTS

THE FRANCISCAN CHARISM
IN THE CHURCH

Introduction

RESPONSE AND REPETITION

OF HIMSELF man is unable to explain the problems of his universe. This does not refer to the phenomena which impinge upon him as a sensory-perceptual organism. On the contrary, despite his growing scientific knowledge, man retains his anxiety about a possible framework within which phenomena occur. Orderliness, interpersonal relationships, sanction, immortality, priority of values—each man individually imposes a framework according to his struggles and his lights.

This framework can and has been derived by some men without reference to a transcendent being. Others are led—or often driven—by a variety of arguments to affirm the existence of a Creator as the source and ground of their framework. But every such affirmation must be a unique statement by each person who makes it. The *assent* of the mind to a divine principle of one's being never occurs without a simultaneous *consent* of the will. More accurately, the *whole person* chooses to understand the universe in the special light of faith, generally with an emotional dimension of exhilaration, or relief, or even foreboding. In this sense faith is not communicable between men; it can barely even be described.

The broadest notion of faith is a trusting response to another person's superior experience. Only when knowledge is integrated into behavior does it become *experience*. The believer, persuaded by another's credentials, replaces his inexperience with knowledge that can be observed and verified in another's actions.

With respect to religious faith, a man is constrained to search out the person of superior experience or he comes upon one who claims to possess it.

Even the persons who have been indoctrinated in a particular religious faith from childhood must seek out or be converted by the testimony of another's superior experience of God. As adults they must give assent and consent to the doctrines and values of their creed. By its nature faith includes a certain submission. Mohammed made this concept central to belief in his message; *Islam* means "submission." The immediate consequence of faith is a relative security and awareness of purpose in the universe, based on God's intervention in human history through those men who are open to the divine communications.

But the sense of security and purpose is merely a placebo, a rationalization, and a cowardly escape from human striving, unless a fundamental motive force, stemming from man's own nature, is concomitant with faith. This motive force is not supernatural in itself, nor is it a cause of faith. It is, rather, a *catalyst* typically present with *mature* faith. This catalyst appears to be threefold: man's awareness of his own perfectibility, his aspiration to encompass all the world in his mind, and his drive to experience whatever is possible to the human state. Of course, inasmuch as God uses many means to sanctify man, a theologian would see these natural qualities as "actual graces" to the degree that they developed under divine inspiration.

Further, it is the balanced and flexible personality with a goodly tolerance of ambivalence which can take the risk of faith and remain poised at the juncture of the city of God and the city of man. Or rather, the man of faith consciously attempts to make the two cities coextensive with each other. For him, the perfectibility of man and his desire to experience whatever exists is never accomplished without an investigation of others' claims to knowledge of the transcendent God and his immanent manifestations.

God reveals himself in many ways according to the condition and conditioning of men in their evolutionary struggle. Each self-revelation of God, if it is a genuine one, remains forever valid. Although God is simple and uncluttered by nature, man both as an individual and as a member of a social group understands God slowly—through an accumulation of insights and relationships. Thus the God of the Old Testament gave the supreme commandment to love him and one's neighbor quite explicitly. Nevertheless the Israelites understood the mode of loving God and the identity of one's neighbor rather narrowly until the prophets and subsequent leaders expanded the meaning of these relationships.

For Christians the fullness of God's self-exposure is the Word-made-flesh, Jesus Christ. He claimed the unique experience of being totally human and absolutely divine. As a prophet he also revealed this slowly and cumulatively, allowing his listeners then and now to absorb the communication by degrees. The person who searches for God during his adult years, if he intends to share in the Christian experience, must sooner or later be evangelized. That is, he must listen to the claims of Christ and submit himself, realizing that he is ignorant of the full relationship he might have with God.

Christ, moreover, shows himself as the son of God in the denotative sense of having the same nature. In the religions which existed prior to Christ, sonship was not an uncommon concept, but the term was merely connotative. Nevertheless, the connotations of providential care and individual interest were also very precise dimensions of Christ's teaching about the divine paternity. Yet no one, Christ asserted, comes to the Father (in this full sense) unless the Son reveals him. In the third strophe of the Prologue to St. John's Gospel, the writer tells us, "Any who did accept him he empowered to become children of God. These are they who believe in his name" (verse 12). In the fifth strophe the author proclaims Christ's unique and superior experience: "No one has ever seen God. It is God, the only Son, ever at his Father's side, who has revealed him" (verse 18).

To sum up this introduction we can say that the Christian believer *responds* submissively—not cravenly—to Christ's claim to know the heavenly Father from the experience of his own sonship. The community of those who believe in him, that is, the Church of Christ, is the continuation of his mission to the world. The believer with mature faith and therefore integral personality attempts to enter into and *repeat* the experience of Christ as the Son of God. According to their natural talents and supernatural gifts the members of the Christian community struggle to extend the personality and mission of Christ among men. Such is the context into which we must place all activities of Christian believers. This, of course, includes religious life in all of its forms. *Response* and *repetition* are the key words of faith in God through Jesus Christ.

Chapter I

CHARISM EVOLVES FROM BAPTISM

IN THE BIBLE, that continually expanding self-revelation of God, we see a double phenomenon evolve in the community of God. This phenomenon is the mode by which God involves himself in the lives of those who are accessible to his communications. The mode creates a polarity, rather than a dichotomy within the mission of the Temple and of the Church.

On one hand, there developed a very formal and ritualistic structure to be the ordinary liaison between God and man. This was the levitical priesthood serving the altar of the Temple, coupled—at a later date—with the worship of the local congregation in the synagogue. In the theocratic framework of Israel the religious leaders were often political leaders and judges as well.

On the other hand, we read of the non-hierarchical expressions of the religious community. Such were the schools of prophetism, sometimes under the guidance of a well-known mouthpiece of God, who was a kind of *guru* to his followers. Discovery of the Qumran Scrolls, moreover, bears witness to the existence of groups similar to Christian religious orders in many respects, but also like the mystery cults popular in the Near East. Groups like the Essenes proposed to live a life that intensified the ordinary commitment to Israel's covenant with God. In addition to these currents within Judaism that thrived independently of, yet not divorced from the Temple, there were the nazirites. Samson and John the Baptist come to mind; they were dedicated to the ascetical and at times to the eremitical life. They hearkened back to the Israelites in Exodus, wandering as the Spirit dictated, dependent upon the largesse of nature, and rather isolated in purification from the earthbound people surrounding them. The prophets, whether so ascetical or not, more directly involved themselves in the spiritual life of the total community, serving as points of contact with God apart from the hierarchy. Their "schools" were probably the training ground for popular preachers and mystical theologians. Such schools were in contrast to the rabbinical schools, like that of Gamaliel, under whom St. Paul studied. The latter groups were oriented to official religion, the canons of Judaism, and the dogmatic interpretation of the Scriptures and prescriptions of behavior for the believer.

The history of the Old Testament reveals the manifold religious life within the ancient covenant. As Christians recite in the Creed, they express their belief in "the Holy Spirit, the Lord and Giver of life, who spoke through the prophets." The structures of Judaism were constantly being renewed or "updated" by the inspiration of the Spirit of God, breathing where it chose. This self-revelation of God to individual prophets, nazirites, and founders of religious groups is the personal *charism* or insight that individual possessed—or rather, which possessed him. This charism was the source of the individual's *enthusiasm*, a word which means "God within" or "within God."

It would be a grave error to make too sharp a division or separation between the hierarchy of Israel and charismatic persons, as though these were completely separate entities. The proper concept is rather one of polarization, whereby the interests and values of one group often are in tension with those of the other. But we must remain aware that any member of either group, that is, any member of God's community, could and can receive a charism. Historically, many of the formal rituals and behavioral prescriptions developed by charismatic persons were adopted by the hierarchy and even imposed in a crystallized form upon the universal membership. (A case in point is auricular confession of sins, introduced by Christian monks in the early Middle Ages among those whom they evangelized.) Members of the hierarchy of Israel, in order to be effective, would also have been the vehicles of a personal charism, if they were alert to it. This was their "grace of office."

The analogies between religious expression in the Temple and in the Church are readily apparent. The Spirit of God addresses himself to every accessible person. In the new covenant that same Spirit quickens the Body of Christ. St. Paul analyzed the multiple charisms in his local foundations. Individuals were given gifts to preach, to nurse, to educate, to speak in and interpret glossolalia. The spiritual gift was joined to the natural talent of an individual. Most important was the use of the gift for the benefit of and with the approval of the community. As in Israel, the charism need not put its possessors in opposition to the hierarchy, for charism belongs to the hierarchy as well as to others; bishops and theologians, for example, have their own charisms. We might say that the supreme charism of truth resides in the Bishop of Rome to the degree that he is accessible to the operations of the Spirit.

The centuries of the Church's existence have given rise to many specialized individual and group experiences parallel to those of Israel. Whether these experiences were uniquely personal or pertained to an entire religious movement, they were intensifications of the covenant of sonship proposed in the Gospel. Religious founders made their *response* of faith go beyond what Christians typically vow in baptism. Although every Christian is obliged to seek perfection through the evangelical counsels of poverty, chastity, and obedience, founders of religious orders and their adherents propose to *intensify* their baptismal vow. They usually make a public commitment, acceptable to the Church, to *repeat* the life of Christ in a pattern suited to the temper and needs of their times. This is their charism. It is a gift that stands in peril of extinction once it has become linked to an institutional framework. But, once again it must be emphasized, the polarities of "objectivized" communication from God through ordinary, even bureaucratic channels and the "subjectivized" inspiration received extraordinarily by individuals should not be understood too rigidly. Every charism must be consonant with the mission of the Church. On the other hand, without the innovative direction supplied by charismatic persons to the body politic, the Church would remain static, inflexible, condemned to ossification.

All Christians, as we said, are bound to perfection. This commitment is convalidated by pronouncing one's baptismal vow—or at least by the mature recognition of the implications of baptism as an adult. In this sense even "born Catholics" need evangelization, which ideally should occur before the sacrament of Confirmation. (Perhaps some of the religious and priests who gravitated into their state of life without such an adult confrontation with Christ are among those who are leaving their ministry in the time of crisis.)

To "come to perfection as your heavenly Father is perfect" (Matt. 5:48), as the New Testament states, has the meaning of being "complete" or "integral" as a person by becoming a son or daughter of God. Grace, which is a share in the Trinitarian life of God, uniquely provides this experience. Thus the man of faith repeats the life of or reincarnates Christ upon earth. This repetition is contingent upon the life style which one chooses or to which one is conditioned by his personal history. The Christian struggle lies in making Christ present to the community, and to the world at large according to one's own perceptions.

The different expressions of religious life in the various orders, as well as outside the framework of an institute, are all individual charisms that bespeak the continuing response of faith. Each expression needs the approval of the believing community to ensure its value. Typically the hierarchy voices its approval as the spokesman for the community. Nevertheless, many new charisms in the Church had to struggle for years and prove their relevance before they were recognized as coming from the Spirit. Even when members of the hierarchy were insensitive, however, the work of God could not be stopped, as long as the possessors of the charism were attuned to the divine communication. Whereas "official" or institutional approval may have been tardy, the validity of the charism was implemented by the non-official community, which was being built up by the charism. If the official leaders were uncomfortable, it was because they have the serious obligation to preserve and balance the enduring aspects of Church life. The very notion of "balance" connotes a precarious condition. Although St. Vincent de Paul and St. Francis de Sales, for example, tried to keep their concept of unstructured religious life viable, their foundations were nevertheless trapped into existing frameworks. When St. Francis of Assisi proposed his mobile and uncluttered rule of Gospel life to the Pope, the latter was unwilling to approve until a Cardinal pointed out that refusing approval was tantamount to denying that the life of Christ could be relived.

Despite the paragraph above, one cannot avoid the canonical ideal of a vocation as being a "call" from lawful Church superiors who stand in the place of God when they accept individuals into a new status within the Body of Christ. Ultimately this approval is what differentiates the religious from the typical Christian. Certainly anyone or any group can propose to live the Gospel life in an intensified way. But the religious are to *exhibit an official example of how a community of Christians—or just one Christian—makes Christ present to the world.* This modality of official approval historically has become an essential note of religious life as a charism within God's people. As we read in Section 45 of *Lumen Gentium,* the document of the Second Vatican Council on the mystery of the Church, religious life is essentially the public profession of the evangelical counsels.

Although religious life, as it is presently lived, *typically* includes the taking of vows and living the common life, its foundation is the *public profession* of the counsels. Therefore, isolates (such as exclaustrated religious) and so-called "lay" religious, who do not live the common life, are true religious even in the canonical sense. The term "public" means that the Church officially recognizes the individual or group to be professors of the Gospel life. Thus a person who promises before a bishop or his delegate to live the evangelical counsels is officially a religious, even if the promise were to have been made in secret. The consequence is that the official Church assumes the obligation to provide spiritual direction for that person's spiritual growth and engagement in the divinely ordained mission of the Church. Conversely, a person who stands before a thousand others and promises to live the Gospel life, but without official recognition of this charism, is still professing the counsels privately. Naturally, it goes without saying, private profession may be most perfect, pleasing to God, and with sacramentality for the believing community. The person who makes such a promise may be considered a "free-lance" religious without a title to the Church's direction any more special than the Christian who made no such profession.

Because the profession of the counsels may be made and lived even without oath-taking, vows as such do not appear to be an essential of the religious state. Thus Franciscan "secular" tertiaries can share in the charism of religious life without pronouncing vows. Nor do we have any record that all the early virgins, hermits, or ascetics bound themselves by vows. It is apparent that many of them, if not most, lived no common life. The virgins generally stayed with their families. Yet the Church gave recognition to their lives by assigning them a special place during the community worship. Theirs was a modality of the Gospel life that received the approval of the hierarchy.

Chapter Six of *Lumen Gentium* points out that the Church regulates and establishes enduring forms for interpreting poverty, chastity, and obedience (Section 43). The religious state is not a midpoint between the clergy and laity, but rather draws its members from both groups (Section 43). Religious divorce themselves from obstacles that hinder the fervor of charity and divine worship, so that they can devote themselves to the welfare of the entire Church (Section 44). They thereby become a sign that attracts others to fulfill their Christian vocations; they become an eschatological sign of the Church in the glory of perfected love (Section 44). As has been said above, religious life as a charism is outside the hierarchy, yet brings it new life (Section 44). The religious institute's particular insight into the Gospel is the source of its special energy or enthusiastic joy.

Because single or group religious life represents an intensification of the baptismal vow, it does not belong to its members alone. The whole Church, after official recognition, becomes aware of the charism and is concerned about that form of the Christ-life. (Analogously, the whole Church is interested in celibacy as an adjunct to the priesthood, because the priesthood of Christ, according to St. Peter's Epistle, is shared in by all the baptized.) Nevertheless, even though the metamorphosis of an institute's external works, prayer life, and customs falls under the jurisdiction of the hierarchy, only the possessors of the charism can appraise the validity of the changes. For this reason the recent Vatican Council alerted religious foundations to recover the spirit of their founders. But what of those institutes which decide that their lives need a complete overhauling, in order to keep their charism viable, and yet to whom the hierarchy does not grant leave? They must first of all be obedient to God, remove themselves from officialdom, and courageously "reduce" themselves from an approved institute, and search for their identity as a "free-lance" group. Perhaps at some future date they may seek the seal of approval again. It is a sad thought, however, that the institutional Church is not large enough to garner into its framework all the life styles of religious life, because charism is a "many-splendored thing."

Members who are indifferent to updating their special spirit are actually betraying their institute. Traditions should be reverenced without being irrevocably canonized. The spirit of the charism gives life, but external forms can become oppressive. Now religious institutes—including their "lay" affiliates, as Third Order fraternities—are urged to trace their spiritual ancestry back to Christ, but through their founders, who were communicated a special gift of understanding the Christ-life.

Any life style chosen by a Christian can be the best way for him to respond to and repeat the life of Christ begun in baptism. In their particular pattern, religious seem to have caught the parallels between baptismal and religious profession. The local community scrutinizes its potential members and subjects them to a catechumenate before initiation. Witnesses for the community attest to the candidates' worthiness and sponsor the new members as they pronounce their credo. The latter are given a badge or garment to token their "putting on the new man."

St. Louis IX of France, patron of tertiaries, sensed that his Franciscan status grew out of his baptism. He often signed himself "de Poissy," because he had been baptized at that place.

Chapter **II**

RECOVERING THE FRANCISCAN CHARISM

WE READ IN CHAPTER EIGHT of the First Book of Samuel that the elders of Israel approached the prophet and asked him to set a king over them. After all, he was old and his two sons left much to be desired in their judgeship. Even though Yahweh was not entirely pleased, he told Samuel to listen to the voice of the people. Samuel, having no sympathy with the "new breed," warned the Israelites against their "secularism." They wanted to be like other nations. Nevertheless, when the kingship was established, it brought a clearer identity to God's community, and the kings proved to be not notably worse than some of the judges and high priests. The secular tendency and involvement with the world ultimately brought Judaism to its greatest national fruitfulness. Nor did the Jews lose their charism as the chosen people.

Religious orders should remain, like Israel of old, in a constant state of growth and re-formation. Those who possess a charism must be flexible enough to preserve it without obscuring it with the accretions which may merely have been temporary safeguards. In an address to leaders of religious orders on May 23, 1964, Pope Paul VI reminded them that they would remain prosperous only to the degree that their way of life and activities remain under the inspiration of their founders. So Dominicans are struggling with the self-concept of contemplative apostles. Carmelites wish to test whether the eremitical life of solitude is consistent with

15

priestly-ministerial labors.[1] The Jesuits are reexamining their function as a missionary institute and creators of small, first-rate liberal arts colleges. Benedictines wonder how stability of place and their origin as a lay movement fit into the mobility of modern life. Assuredly the canonical grant of exemption exists to allow religious institutes to foster their charisms, which the local Ordinary could not be expected to understand in his assignments within the diocese. Some theologians surprisingly wish to make religious priests only members of the diocesan presbyterate. It is alleged that religious orders are at times divisive, since their members move freely from one diocese to another without long-range allegiance to the projects of the local Ordinary. Thus the argument runs that either religious orders of men should be suppressed altogether, or they should be totally controlled in their assignments by the bishop of the diocese. No doubt the Church is best served when religious clergy cooperate closely with and join the diocesan presbyterate for the sake of collegial processes in those areas where religious are affected. But the mission of religious is received uniquely from the Bishop of Rome, who is the focus of the Church's universal mission. Thus even the religious *priests*—not only Sisters and Brothers—need canonical exemption for mobility and service within the Church universal. If religious institutes, particularly those of men, would actually begin to revitalize their mission to the Church, their critics would have less cause to comment with the old cliché that religious take the vows and the diocesan priests observe them.

There are not a few scandals or "stumbling blocks" within the Franciscan Order as well. The First Order has been divided into three groups, which in some instances are even hostile to one

---

[1] See the article by Brocard Sewell, O. Carm., "Black and White Friars: A Common Crisis," in *The Clergy Review*, New Series, LII (December, 1967), 969-976. Fr. Bede Edwards, O. D. C., responds to this article in the March, 1968, issue "Correspondence," Vol. LIII, pages 225-227.

another. The Second Order seemed unable to reconcile divergent elements and splintered into reform groups. The "regular" religious of the Third Order, particularly the Sisters, have not been commonly aware of their share in a specifically Franciscan charism. The "lay" members of the Third Order often cannot find First Order priests to form them into dynamic fraternities.

Nevertheless, all three orders presumably participate in the same renewal of the Christ-life among men that originated with St. Francis of Assisi. He himself remarked, "The order is a very large society, which is like a worldwide convention joining together in a single life style" (Celano, *Second Life*). One purpose of this study is to clarify the Franciscan charism as the common focus to which all the jurisdictions of the threefold order can look. Some day charity and flexibility may be so common in the order that some kind of unity and closer awareness of each other will result. What began as a division within the First Order over involvement with the world or sequestration from it has lost its meaning in the post-Vatican-II era; involvement is inescapable for active religious. Within each of the Three Orders the life style of one jurisdiction is not unlike the others. And in those few areas where differences are not so minimal, one would think that the order would be so open a society that the different levels of aspiration could coexist without the multiplication of bureaucracies.

St. Francis was keenly aware of his revolutionary charism (which apparently has been ossified by monastic calcification). "I do not want you to cite me any other rule—not St. Augustine's, nor St. Bernard's, nor St. Benedict's. The Lord told me to become a new type of simpleton in the world. God did not choose to lead me along any other path than the way of experience" (*Legenda Antiqua*). We read in another early biography of his distress over monastic or eremitical currents during his lifetime: "I love my brothers to the degree I am able. Were they to follow my path, I would love them all the more and not alienate myself from them. There are some superiors who are drawing the brothers into different ways after the example of the ancient religious. These men are inattentive to my instructions, but what they are attempting will become obvious in the future" (Celano, *Second Life*). Perhaps it has taken seven centuries for us to become fully aware of the saint's prediction. For his brothers St. Francis called his *Rule* their "book of life, the hope of our salvation, the collateral of our glory, the marrow of the Gospel, our way of the cross, the state of perfection, our key to paradise, the guarantee of our eternal testament" (*The Mirror of Perfection*).

Perhaps one explanation of the division within the order is the ancient Latin aphorism *quot capita tot sententiae*—there are as many opinions about the Franciscan charism as there are persons reflecting upon it. Each concept is likely to spawn a different life style to keep it intact. In each case the problem is to preserve the charism without overwhelming it. As has been said above, the life style of an order is related to its charism, or subjective insight, whereby members convalidated their divine sonship within the institutional framework of the Church, which is the normative, objective channel of communication with our heavenly Father. If one does not insist too narrowly upon the analogies, charism and institution are like body and soul, rudder and sail, limits and self-expression. Even within the order's expression of its charism, a similar polarization tends to develop in order to keep alive and interpret the original life style with precise regulations.

Each institute renews Christ's presence on earth corporately. As every Christian "puts on Christ," so the institute assumes a dimension of the personality of Christ in a way proper to itself. As a social reincarnation of Christ, it becomes a special sign to its lay affiliates or those members of the Mystical Body committed to its spiritual care. Some charisms seem clear: the hermits, the teachers, the nurses, the preachers of Christ crucified, those who orient their lives to the Blessed Sacrament, and so forth. Some institutes seem to have arisen to serve local, sometimes transitory spiritual and social needs. In time they fall into desuetude and perish. For those who have the courage to phase themselves out of existence or merge with others, their "reward in heaven is great" (Matt. 5:12).

Basing themselves, therefore, on the insights of their founder, Franciscans must specify and clarify their corporate personality or risk losing their identity—and perhaps usefulness—to the Church and to the world. They must distinguish themselves from foundations which have a similar life style. St. Francis warned St. Clare against those whose teaching or counsel might lead her from her life style and especially from poverty. In his *Testament*, a kind of farewell address to the order, he once again insisted that the life his brothers were to lead was revealed to him by God alone and was not derived from other religious institutes.

Up to this point, the words "charism," "life style," "religious life," and "corporate personality" have not been precisely differentiated from each other. "Charism" is a general term that indicates a *personal gift* of the Spirit, used for the good of the Church. If it receives approval from the hierarchy, the charism is said to participate in the official mission of the Church to make Christ present in the world. "Religious life" is an "official" charism that represents an *intensified response* of faith to one's baptismal commitment to repeat the life of Christ. "Life style" is the particular *external manifestation* of the Christ-life chosen by an individual or institute. "Personality," finally, refers to the *internal spirit* of the institute, as evidenced by emphasis on certain virtues, certain limits or (conversely) freedom for self-expression, and above all a well-defined self-concept.

One can oppose "personality" to "essence" in defining the spirit of an institute. The latter term is too inflexible, categorized, dogmatic. It is a static statement of the order's function in the Mystical Body. "Personality," on the other hand, is an existential term. It is a dynamic statement of the order's place in the Church. "Personality" arises from the insights and experiences of the order's members. It defines itself according to the perceptions of its members. It admits degrees and potentials not yet specified. This is one of the important principles upon which the rest of these chapters is based.

There is no doubt that the personality of a founder or foundress influences the subsequent evolution of the order's personality corporately considered. Whereas this is inevitable and even necessary, the two personality concepts are not perfectly interchangeable. Thus the image of St. Francis singing along with the swallows, his hands filled with daisies, and trailed by the rabbits and wolves, is not necessarily compatible with the life style of all his followers. But the freedom to be himself, however silly it might appear to others, is definitely an aspect of St. Francis that is inseparable from his enduring legacy to his sons and daughters, lay or religious.

An amusing anecdote from the pages of early Franciscan history recalls how the simple Brother Juniper aped St. Francis in such personal habits as coughing when the latter coughed, spitting when he did, and so forth. The annalist made the point, of course, that imitation of the Seraphic saint referred to his spiritual qualities, and prayer life. Whereas no one today is likely so slavishly to copy such actions, even if they were known after a lapse of seven hundred years, the fact remains that St. Francis is not entirely recoverable from history. His biographers used many legends that obscure the facts, always, we may presume, with good will, but in some cases with biased intent. We read dubious accounts of the saint casting a sick brother out of a house he believed some of his confreres had bought, whereas St. Francis shows special concern for the ailing in his *Rules*. In another account the founder sends Rufino, son of a noble family, naked to preach in the cathedral as a test, whereas St. Francis admonishes his brothers in the *Rules* not to obey a reprehensible command that would be contrary to their conscience. A story in the *Mirror of Perfection* has St. Francis forbidding a novice to have a breviary for prayer, whereas the *Rules* specifically allow a breviary. The well-known anthology *The Little Flowers*, compiled in the fourteenth century, has St. Francis avoiding Elias as a future apostate, whereas Celano's more reliable account of the previous century makes them out to be close friends; in fact, St. Francis appointed Elias the superior of the Holy Land, as well as of the whole order.[2]

As is well known, the second generation of Franciscans were divided into several factions according to how they wished to interpret the *Rule* or *Testament* of the founder. The writers who favored certain concepts of poverty or who resisted the structuring process of Brother Elias emphasized and possibly fabricated those stories that supported their claims or interpretations. When St. Bonaventure, the sixth minister general, collected the *Major Legend* between 1260 and 1263 from eyewitnesses who survived the founder,[3] the collection was acclaimed. In fact, other biographies were no longer allowed to be used, at least officially and in the lessons of the breviary. One purpose of the General Chapter in 1260 at Narbonne was to reconcile those factions in the order which were publishing slanted writings about St. Francis that supported their personal views. Nevertheless, because of the relative paucity of extraordinary events and miracles in the *Major Legend*, St. Bonaventure was induced to garner and publish other, but possibly less well authenticated stories.

---

[2] The reader is referred to the fascinating and scholarly introduction to *The Little Flowers of St. Francis* by Serge Hughes (a Mentor-Omega book: MT-593), published in New York in 1964.

[3] In the Prologue to the *Major Legend*, St. Bonaventure refers to the *familiaribus eius adhuc superviventibus*. As the Quaracchi Editors show, much of the book derives from Celano's writings. The latter, of course, had an even closer contact than St. Bonaventure with the intimates of St. Francis.

Another case in point is the *Book of Conformities* (circa 1385-1390), attributed to Bartholomew of Pisa and written to cite the parallels between the life of St. Francis and the life of Christ—twelve disciples, the stigmata, and so forth. In fact, it is related that when Donna Pica was about to give birth to the future saint, an angel instructed her to have her child in a stable near their home. This story (upon which medieval piety seems to have nourished itself) has recently been disproved by the friars' research in Assisi.[4]

Nevertheless, such stories are not without value in delineating the personality and life style of the saint. Most of them probably grew from some seeds of truth that reveal the kind of impression St. Francis made upon his contemporaries. The purpose of these chapters is not to sift the historical sources. This has been and is being done by experts. The works of St. Francis himself, published by the Quaracchi College, are the primary source, containing the *Rules, Testament,* and other classical writings. Nor is it the purpose of this book to prolong the controversies about the true mind of St. Francis, but to offer the writer's opinion about the separability of St. Francis' personality from that of his order. Perhaps this can serve to bring all Franciscans closer together and provide the Second and Third Orders with a viewpoint on the Franciscan charism which underlies their own approach to God.

Any writer who attempts to distill what is enduring in the personality and life style of St. Francis must be willing to risk the scrutiny of his readers and to expose his own biases and ineptitudes. But the very definition of the "existential personality," as evolving from the members' insights, experiences, and perceptions into potential expressions not yet specified, bespeaks only a tentative blueprint for development. Nevertheless the writer hopes that it is a chart of common aspirations and group objectives, rather than one man's opinion.

---

[4] Giuseppe Abate, O. F. M. Conv., *La casa dove nacque S. Francesco d'Assisi* (Casa Editrice "Oderisi": Gubbio, 1941).

Chapter III

HISTORY AS A CONDITIONER OF CHARISM

THE TERM "HISTORY" is used here in a twofold sense. A person develops within the unique milieu of the emotional tone of his home life, the structure of his family, his developmental rate, his personal education, the traumatic events of his youth, and so on. Secondly, a person is the product of his times, its politics, its prejudices, its superstitions, its peculiar ethos.

The personal history of St. Francis brings to mind his flair for the dramatic, a decidedly romantic view of life, a desire to be his "own man" against the options of his father, and, no doubt, some grandiose ideas of his own future greatness—all of which, had he failed, would have provided just another case in a psychology text. It is important to analyze these factors in his personality in order to compare them with the "existential personality" of his foundation, the three orders and their subdivisions.

It took many sober confrontations with hunger, mockery, and alienation from his fellows to make Francis more realistic. Nevertheless he did not lose his gaiety, freedom of expression, and aspiration to change the whole world. When theoreticians dissect a saint's life in behavioristic or psychoanalytic literature, they provide a real service to those who follow the saint, even if some of their underlying theoretical models have to be rejected. Whereas these personal case studies are invaluable, there is always the peril that a vocation might be reduced to a merely natural phenomenon. A vocation, however—an inexplicable mystery—is also a supernatural gift. A charism cannot be quantified; it is

23

more (at least to the believer) than a career choice, although it is also that, inasmuch as a charism can be rejected because of a human agent's inaccessibility to the Spirit. A vocational charism is a profound and continuing engagement of the person with God; it is locked up in that rapport which is the communication of the self—both the divine and the human self. People who have been in love can understand. Nevertheless, to the degree that the ego needs of a person can be scrutinized, the natural processes bound up in a charism are subject to description.

Throughout the history of the mystical life of the community of God, we see that certain qualities are attributed to certain saints, not only inseparably from their names, but also as if their heroic virtue had been founded upon a particular quality. There was the seraphic St. Teresa of Avila, the soldierly St. Ignatius Loyola, the serene St. Francis de Sales, the "little" St. Thérèse of Lisieux, the chaste St. Aloysius, the poor and humble Man of Assisi. As the theologians like to assert, the possession of one virture to a heroic degree perforce includes all the others. Whereas such heroism may, indeed, be a legacy to a saint's followers, one cannot assume that a single virtue is the totality of a charism handed on to a whole religious institute. Each saint presumably practices all the virtues as occasions present themselves and according to the level of his spiritual development.

Before applying these ideas to the personality of St. Francis, it is necessary to comment on a broader historical context of a person's philosophy of life. As the Roman annalist Tacitus succinctly remarked in his classic epigram: "Strengths of character are most accurately measured in the light of the era which most easily gave them rise."

The *theological background* of a saint may give him a prejudice as easily as an insight. It is said that St. Francis Xavier told the Japanese that their ancestors were in hell. When St. Francis of Assisi wrote his *First Rule*, containing his authentic thought, he directed his missionary brothers to avoid contentions and disputes and to be subject to every human being. Then they were to announce the word of God, if it appeared pleasing to the Lord. When the five protomartyrs of the order preached in North Africa, apparently they announced that Mohammed and his followers were the minions of the devil—which is not a very ecumenical observation. We remember that St. Paul the Apostle himself had to revise his thinking as he slowly realized that he was not, after all, living in the last few years of the Church with Christ's reappearance imminent.

A saint's personal *asceticism* reflects a relationship to the existing economic level or standard of living. Self-discipline must be more stringent than the average way of life to count for mortification. Yet the lower middle classes of the twentieth century— or even many of the poor receiving public aid—live in greater abundance, variety, and physical security than the wealthy of the twelfth century. Asceticism, therefore, may not be wholly interpreted outside the reference of its historical milieu and the customs of the time. Above all, asceticism has no meaning outside the context of its motivation, which can change from century to century.

The *scientific knowledge* of an age tends to color its philosophical currents. Thus the Middle Ages were distrustful of tampering with nature or delving into such "diabolical" arts. Even the good Franciscan Roger Bacon was imprisoned for experiments common today in grammar school. Past concepts of geography so limited men's horizons that during the medieval period, for example, missionary ventures to dim, distant lands seemed unimportant or impossible—at least prior to Franciscan and Dominican excursions to Tartary even before the Polos. In our own time we see religious persons eschew the findings of the behavioral sciences that can aid spiritual and psychological maturation. The scientific study of ancient literatures, religions of the world, and anthropology casts light upon the meanings of Sacred Scripture that otherwise knowledgeable and religious men and women are reluctant to accept.

The *political and nationalistic tendencies* of some eras left their mark also on religious orders. Up to our own time we read the constitutions of some orders which exclude Catholics of Jewish extraction from entering their ranks without demeaning "dispensations." Monarchical structures that smack of the "divine right of kings" and militaristic regimes that form members into unthinking robots who plant cabbages upside down at a command have fostered a concept of law that reflected the thinking of the leaders rather than the aspirations of all the members.

The *personal idiosyncrasies* of a founder or saint often rise out of his environment. Some considered bathing too sensual, halitosis a sign of an evil interior disposition, and any kind of humor an insult to the suffering Christ (of whom it is not recorded in the Gospel that he ever laughed). One would not cavil, of course, at St. Paul of the Cross, who wore no hat out of respect for the omnipresent God—if the story is true—because he did not impose his personal asceticism upon his followers. Also, the forms of prayer and meditation that succeeded for a foundress may have been bequeathed to subsequent generations of followers, simply because they were commonly accepted norms in a past century. The accretions of the *devotio moderna* are a case in point. Some types of Marian devotion, a certain sentimentality in prayers, and sacred art forms that distract rather than edify are examples of other personal viewpoints that can be thrust upon a whole institute. To all these environmental factors that condition a religious founder must be added the human ones: spiritual directors who may have been insensitive to the nature of the charism, manipulatory bishops and pastors who needed personnel to fill a local need not related to the charism, and the influence upon a founder or foundress who lived temporarily with an already existing religious institute.

The melodramatic dimension of St. Francis' personality, for example, caused him to strip before the townspeople of Assisi and return even his clothes to his natural father, so that thereafter he might call God alone his father. Another time he expressed a desire to have even the walls of houses smeared with meat on Christmas, so that they might "feast" in commemoration of the Lord's birth. He directed his brothers to collect any scrap on which the name of the Lord had been written and discarded, lest it be walked upon. The General Chapter, however, counter-manded St. Francis. It is shallow theology lightly to attribute such actions — assuming they are all historical events—to the indwelling Spirit of a saint.

In any case, these excesses were on the periphery of St. Francis' personality and do not represent a significant dimension of his life any more than the odd actions every human being occasionally performs. These extraordinary acts were relatively rare in St. Francis' life when set into the broad sweep of his life style. Such things are not essential to following him, except insofar as they reveal a transparent and spontaneous person who was not fearful of exposing his emotional life. They appear in the literature for the obvious reason that such material makes better reading than the daily, monotonous, earthbound commitment to prayer, work, and normal asceticism.

This distinction must be made in the personality of St. Francis as well as in the struggle of the first Franciscans to achieve a corporate identity or charism. For example, St. Francis gave St. Anthony permission to study and teach the brothers sacred theology. This must have presumed a desire for learning on their part, even though St. Francis in his *Second Rule* warns the unlettered brothers not to be *anxious* to acquire learning. Later on, St. Bonaventure's theological work *De reductione omnium artium ad theologiam* subsumes all human learning under some aspect of sacred science. As the order continues to clarify its self-concept by its activities, it will continue to research the theological dimension of psychology, literature, science, the cinema, and so forth. Yet St. Francis might have forbidden analogous activities to his contemporary brothers.

We see history affecting other divisions of Franciscandom as well. Tertiaries at one time took vows even though they lived with their families. Unfortunately this appeared too fluid a state for religious life in the minds of the hierarchy, and as time passed, the secular Third Order became in effect another of countless parochial organizations. The monasticizing of the Poor Clares is another case close at hand. It seems to be alien to the Franciscan spirit to prevent truly human engagement and apostolic availability by placing curtains and grilles between the Clares and visitors or clients of the household. It is appalling to realize that, except for those Second Order convents which are beginning to adapt, a member can go to the parlor to visit only in the presence of another Sister; that she can never give her family a kiss and embrace; that she is not even allowed to see others' faces. This was certainly not the life style between St. Francis and St. Clare themselves. The *Rule* of the Poor Clares was approved on August 9, 1253, by Pope Innocent IV. But St. Francis never wrote a *Rule* for them himself; it was as if he were yet trying to determine a life style consonant with the Gospel. Perhaps he could not reconcile the strict enclosure that women typically experienced with his own free spirit. Nevertheless he wholeheartedly approved the Poor Clares' poverty as compared with the wealth of some women's monasteries.

Even for his own brothers St. Francis wrote two *Rules*[1] and a final *Testament* before he died—all of which shows how slowly a charism is clarified, even to its possessor at times. As the order passed from the patriarchal government of St. Francis to the

---

[1] Some scholars refer to the *three Rules* of St. Francis. The first, however, was merely a collection of Scriptural quotations. Francis thought that the Bible was a sufficient guide for a friar. He was pressed later to comment

senatorial government of General Chapters, the Franciscan charism underwent transformation as to the external life style required to support it. There is an analogy with the Apostolic Age of the Church. The direct rule of Christ and the mobility of the Twelve gave way to stabilized churches in many localities, from which the Apostles returned, as on the occasion of the first General Council at Jerusalem. The primitive Church derived its own self-concept slowly, without (as we think) losing its Christianity; the same process was verified in primitive Franciscanism. And in both groups, as it says in the Acts of the Apostles, a "bitter contention" arose among the members. The followers of St. Peter—who was, indeed, a Pope—lost to the faction of St. Paul, which saw the Gospel life, even one generation after Christ, as not being bound to a literal following of Jesus in such matters as purification, circumcision, and Temple worship. Each reader can draw his own conclusions.

---

on how these quotations might be applied to his own century. His commentary became the *First Rule* to be written down; this occurred in 1221. Because it was not presented to the Holy See for written approval, it is known as the *non-bullata*, that is, "without a papal bull." The *Second Rule* represents the effort of St. Francis two years later, in 1223, to shorten his previous effort, particularly by deleting many of the Bible quotations and substituting pithy remarks about practical matters such as preaching, elections, the missions, the garb, and so forth. Because this *Second Rule* was given official approval in a papal bull, it is known as the *bullata*.

Chapter IV

THE FIRST FRANCISCAN

ST. FRANCIS LIVED in an age of growing materialism. Historians may have overdrawn the corruption of the diocesan priesthood, the withdrawal of monks from the arena of the world, and the spiritual indifference of lay Catholics, in order to contrast the saint more sharply with his times. Nevertheless, it was certainly a fact that the age was torn by wars, communes were asserting independence from feudal lords, the wealth of monasteries seemed to have little in common with the poor. Usurious practices, the attitude of the newly rising merchant classes, and the seeking of benefices by the clergy did not reflect the principles of the Gospel. The *minores*, or lower classes, whom we would call the disenfranchised today, were only second-rate citizens, without full civil rights. The institutional Church was unable to cope with a situation for which it was also responsible in part. So the Holy Spirit breathed a new charism into the Church through the instrumentality of the Man from Assisi.

This was a man who led no armies, except the spiritual shock troops of a new movement. He wrote no profound or scholarly works, only a few letters and the *Rules* which he called the marrow of the Gospel. His financial empire was grounded on the providence of God and the economy of poverty. He was an unprepossessing figure, rather homely, of a slight build, unfit for athletic honors, save in running the good race and winning the laurel of divine glory. He developed no theory of personality or therapeutic psychology, but simply proposed an example of the imitation of Christ as a panacea for man's problems.

On the other hand, St. Francis did not reject the Establishment. He did not denounce the generals, the scholars, the financiers, the athletes, and the ill-starred reformers of his day. He rather owned up to his own weaknesses. I suspect he would not have denounced communism as a political theory (aside from its atheism and violent revolutions), but would have rejoiced that whole nations were idealistically attempting to "share everything in common," as we read of the early Christians (Acts 2:44). The hippies and beatniks, who hold him as a kind of patron saint, would not have been condemned for their odd rejection of the world's values. But St. Francis would have offered them his alternate plan to change the world's values.

The growth that preceded his total decision for Christ was drawn out for several years. He lived in confusion and in alienation from men and women he had cherished in his earlier life, but he kept faith that his Master would provide a better friendship. A leap from one sort of life into another wholly unlike it was precarious for him as well as it would be for any man. That divine grace is present does not mean that the human struggle is absent; the one generally triggers the other. Each added insight was born of lonely reflection upon himself. He was a pragmatic person, who knew that, if others were to have faith in his mission, they would have to see that kind of knowledge which is experience. As he was later quoted in the *Mirror of Perfection:* "A person possesses no more knowledge than what is put to practice, just as a religious is a preacher only according to the measure of his actions. The tree is known only by its fruits."

His illness in the jail of Perugia taught Francis the brevity of life. His fever and vision on the road to battle showed him that he was to serve the Lord God, not a warlord. The high life of Assisi, to which he momentarily returned, demonstrated the emptiness of a life lived for pleasure. The months of moody isolation in a cave outside of town led him to abandon himself to the only Caretaker who would not fail to provide every essential need for life here and hereafter. Seeking out beggars to imitate and lepers to kiss tested the degree of his self-conquest. The taunts of the community and the ire of his father reinforced his willingness to suffer the supreme test of his ego, which is the ridicule of those to whom we have exposed our inner convictions and our emotional life. The simplicity with which he was to live out his dream is attested to by the unstudied way in which he accepted the mandate to rebuild San Damiano, not yet aware that the Crucified had a larger task of reconstruction planned for him.

As the chronicler records of this long process of growth, St. Francis began to value himself less. This was not in the sense of despising himself, which can be a sickness as easily as a virtue. For he confidently begged alms, collected stones, and invited others to pay with sweat, as he jocosely said, for rebuilding the Church. Finally at the age of twenty-six, on February 24, 1208, he was startled to hear the Gospel of the feast of St. Matthias as if he had heard it for the first time. "The reign of God is at hand!" (Cf. Matt. 10:7-13.)

In his psychoanalytical study of the Protestant reformer Martin Luther,[1] Erik Erikson points out how creative persons decree a moratorium for themselves, as it were. Their inner selves are cultivated while they often starve themselves socially, erotically, and even nutritionally. Young man Francis did this same thing when he lived in a cave near Assisi. He went to Rome and changed clothes with a beggar to test his ability to identify with the poor. He served lepers and the outcasts of society as a means of starving his sense life, to which he had formerly granted indulgence. This occurred between 1206 and 1208. Meanwhile his father grew more exasperated and his mother more distraught at the fool they had brought into the world.

---

[1] Erik H. Erikson, *Young Man Luther* (New York: Norton, 1962). Cf. page 44.

This starvation and moratorium were as necessary as the poise for balance on a springboard before a perilous high dive. Was this to be another failure? First he had renounced a merchant's career. His businessman father grumbled, but, reliving his own apparently lackluster life in his son's adventures, fitted him out for war. Off the boy went in the spring of 1205 to join Gauthier of Palearis, the Chancellor of Emperor Frederick II, in his wars of succession to the Neapolitan states. When he came back home, tried the party circuit again, and finally crawled away from life into a cave, any parent would have been more than dyspeptic— history has dealt too severely with Pietro Bernardone, the father of St. Francis.

Erik Erikson has drawn the lines of the Oedipal conflict very sharply in the life of Martin Luther. He shows how the elder Luther's arbitrary punishments and imposition of personal goals upon his son were later reflected in the thinking of Luther the theologian. God the Father cannot be pleased by human endeavor; all that human beings can do is blindly believe that the incomprehensible "mood swings" of a father somehow are based on compassion. Luther himself records that he almost ran away from the celebration of his first Mass when, at the beginning of the Canon, he had to address God the Father directly and without a mediating person.[2]

Although many influential men of history give evidence of an Oedipal conflict, the altercation between Pietro and Francis does not seem to fall into this category. It is true that his mother, Donna Pica, lavished abundant affection on the boy. We read that once she released him from the cellar-prison in their home, where his father had confined him during one of his angry episodes. Whether one could conclude that this mother-relationship (opposed, incidentally, by the elder Luther in *his* home)

---

[2] The reader is directed to pages 58, 138, and 221 of Erikson's fascinating book.

occasioned a tender regard for the Mother of God on St. Francis' part later in life is rather arbitrary. In any case, during the childhood, adolescence, and young manhood of our saint, his father gave both financial and emotional support and approval to his son. Unlike Martin Luther, the reformer Francis had no need or desire to challenge the authority of the Church. Further, so accustomed to a happy and consistent relationship with his natural father when he was growing up, St. Francis readily transferred his feelings to his supernatural Father. He was not so self-confident during his personal "moratorium," as might be expected; when he lost his father's good graces, he asked an elderly beggar who accompanied him through Assisi, to bless him if he by chance encountered his father's curses. This symbolic action was useful until he *experienced* the divine fatherliness and could say before the world that having only a Father in heaven sufficed for him. Because of his great joy in religious life, there was no "credibility gap" to his statement.

It is the nature of Christian virtue to consist in a struggle. It is not the quality of heroic virtue to have one's will and senses dead to provocation, but to have them oriented to what is positive, morally acceptable, and even enjoyable. Striking this balance with heroic vigilance is the heart of virtue. Thus St. John of the Cross accurately commented toward the end of his life that his extreme sense-deprivations had so become a way of life that they lost the quality of a virtue. St. Francis seems to have had a "sword of Damocles" hanging over his head all his life, bearing witness to his heroic struggle. Once when erotic thoughts provoked him, he threw himself into the briers. Another time he built figures of a "wife" and "children" in the snow with the comment to his confreres that he might beget children yet if he did not continue the struggle.

Physical ills occurred several times in St. Francis' life, exacerbated by his own fasts and irregular life. His fevers from the abortive military exploit to Perugia, his hemorrhages and ulcers toward the end of his life, his failing eyesight which some phy-sician tried to cure with hot irons, his possible cancer that may have ended his life in his middle forties—these were contributory to a state of health that must have affected his psychological life as well. Biographers mention that "demons" drove him to despair by whispering that there would be no salvation for one who ruined his health with excessive mortification. Later in his life the saint complained that he was beset by devils. When he was at prayer by himself on one occasion, he fancied that someone was creeping up behind him to watch. He imagined that voices shrieked out to him in mockery during mountain storms. He had nightmares of a devil who told him that all was in vain, because Francis would finally belong to him anyway. We cannot tell if these episodes of depression were frequent in the life of a man characterized by his contemporaries as consistently joyful and alert to life. It may be that medieval biographers seized upon the episodes as dramatic and sensational anecdotes. In any case, depressions occur to the best of men; how they handle them is more revelatory of psychic life than that they occur. But they cannot be overlooked in delineating the personality of a saint.

Many of the experiences of young man Francis affected the expression of his charism. When he was still working in his father's shop, he once turned away a beggar who asked an alms for the love of God, because he was in the midst of a sale. He was so ashamed that he ran after the beggar with a generous donation. Later he instructed the brothers never to refuse a re-quest made in the name of the love of God. In his *First Rule*, Chapters Seven and Eight, he set down as law what were really personal clarifications of his charism that he left out of the final *Rule*. He commanded his confreres to receive robbers and thieves into the friary; he had done so with a remarkable change in their lives, even to the point of some joining the order. He permitted the brothers to collect money for their sick members, since he himself had been so plagued by illnesses. In the final *Rule*, however, he reiterated the command to care for the sick brothers, but forbade the taking of money for any reason. He likewise mentions concern for lepers in the *First Rule*—which is a consequence of his personal experiences. This does not appear in the final *Rule*. The latter is not shorter in the number of prescriptions, as a matter of fact; but, rather, the *First Rule* is longer because of the lengthy prayers and quotations from the Scriptures. If St. Francis had lived for another ten years, he might have helped his nascent order to specify its charism even further. Perhaps he would have completed a written rule of life for the Clares and the tertiaries.

The "moratorium" of St. Francis—if not the heroic struggle—ended at the Church of St. Nicholas, April 15, 1208. For a month and a half he had worn a peasant's tunic. He had received his first two confreres. He still had no intention of establishing a religious congregation; his was a simple trio of laymen. In a fashion that makes us uneasy, but in keeping with a medieval practice of discerning God's will or prophesying the future by opening the pages of Scripture or of Virgil's works, the three opened the Gospel book at St. Nicholas three times. If they wanted to be perfect, they had to sell all that they had and give it to the poor. They were to take nothing on their proposed venture. They had to deny themselves in order to follow Christ. It is interesting to observe that the three passages do not actually provide a positive prescription at all. The brothers were told to divest themselves of encumbrances. The life style and "personality" of their charism still had to be researched by experiential knowledge. One can easily apply these same three prescriptions to a monk, a hermit, a canon regular, a consecrated virgin, a layman, and so forth.

Despite St. Francis' own ambivalences, he always maintained that the source of his experience was divine. "As the Lord has truthfully revealed to me, God is going to make us thrive into a great congregation and expand our numbers to the uttermost parts of the earth. For your own good," he told his confreres, "I am constrained to show you what I have seen. Nevertheless I would rather keep silence in this matter, had charity not forced me to tell it to you" (Celano, *First Life*). When he reminisced in his final *Testament*, he reiterated, "After the Lord gave me some brothers, nobody pointed out what I should do. But the Most High himself revealed to me that I should live according to the pattern of the holy Gospel." Insofar as the Scriptures provide the source and inspiration for St. Francis, his innovations are rather to be considered a restoration to a world that had forgotten them.

Chapter V

ST. FRANCIS' CREATIVE EXPRESSION
OF RELIGIOUS LIFE

THREE FACTORS in St. Francis' personality tend to rise
to the surface in any description of his life. First of all, he was
a *non-judgmental and flexible person,* open to the suggestions
of God as he slowly understood them during his two or three
years of self-assessment. Secondly, he learned to be *trusting and
responsive to others' needs* as a result of the approval he had received from significant persons in his life. Thus he was able to
transfer this response easily to God, his heavenly Parent. Finally,
because he had enough self-confidence to take risks and tolerate
frustration, he was *pledged to a continuing struggle,* not only to
achieve heroic virtue in the face of physical and mental anguish,
but also to define his own charism and role within his religious
foundation. This natural maturity was the substratum of his
charism.

The opening paragraphs of this book refer to the "motive
force" of faith as awareness of one's perfectibility and the desire
to actualize oneself by all the human experiences possible, including the metaphysical and transcendental ones. St. Francis ex-
trapolated his own self-concept to include the whole world.
Because the Son of God became the Son of Man, human nature
was eminently perfectible and every human being must be re-
spected and unconditionally regarded without prejudice. This
*optimism about each person's potential to share in God's nature
made him propose the high Gospel ideals* without glossing over

them or reducing their force by some rationalization. This is one of the components of the Franciscan charism.

This idealism was, indeed, a part of the romantic personality of St. Francis, as we observed above. The itinerant troubadours of his age inspired him to be the herald of his Great King. And so he composed and sang religious ballads, especially in French, the language of that land where Jesus Christ was so greatly honored in the Blessed Sacrament. The knights of his day, although scarcely above reproach in their motives for battle, were ideally committed to espouse the cause of the poor, the widows, the undefended. And so he identified easily with these champions in his own objectives. It is not unlikely that the saint, were he alive today, would make a little "soul music" on his guitar or identify with astronauts in a wholly different set of metaphors.

What is probably most engaging about the personality of St. Francis was his *freedom of self-expression in religious matters*. This is the obvious consequence of his trust in God to provide inspirations and in man to accept them wholeheartedly. Whoever was willing to "put on Christ" and embrace the Gospel life could certainly be trusted to find his individual way to God. In that sense St. Francis was a sign to his brothers; they were not to imitate him, except in the sense of being free to become what grace had made of them. Not everyone had to leap naked into snow; not everyone could stop a passing Emperor and tell him to behave; not everyone could stand in a meadow and preach to the birds. But all could come to know God and know themselves, and the "truth would set them free."

St. Francis wished to become *transparent to all men*. He could matter of factly predict the phenomenal expansion of his community and his conversations with God about it with no apparent prejudice to his humility—which is another word for realistic self-evaluation. He could openly indulge his poetic fantasies. He liked the lark because she had a gray habit and cowl, like his brothers, and was satisfied to find a few seeds along the road in exchange for praising God. He was unafraid to be sentimental and to risk others' doubts about his virility (and possibly sanity) by buying a lamb intended for slaughter, because it reminded him of the Lamb of God. He opened his emotional life to the scrutiny of men by asserting, "I cry over the sufferings of the Lord Jesus Christ. In fact, I should not be embarrassed to traverse the world, crying aloud for him" (*Legend of the Three Companions*). His transparency drove him to be utterly honest about his own spiritual life. We read in the *Second Life* by Celano that he wanted everyone to know that he had eaten food prepared with animal fat when he was sick during Lent. He likewise sewed patches on the outside of his tunic to match the fur he had to wear on the inside to protect him from the cold during his illness. The point is that a Franciscan is not necessarily required to copy what may be alien to his own spiritual growth, but rather to present that same kind of transparency to the world. For example, St. Francis begged food to bring to Cardinal Hugolino's table when the latter invited him to dinner. The prelate found this offensive. His guest replied that bringing food which had been begged in imitation of the poor Christ, who had lived from alms in his public life, was also bringing honor to Hugolino himself. To some of us this might sound a little smug and condescending.

As one discovers the components of the Franciscan charism, such as optimism about man's perfectibility, freedom of religious self-expression, transparency of life, and so forth, he cannot escape comparing the facts of history. In time the Franciscan Order fell into a lockstep kind of structure. Aware that individuality and especially the mobility required for self-expression were inhibited by monastic structures, huge institutions, and ritualized behavior, St. Francis envisioned *small and flexible groups of men*—like the twelve Apostles—who could rapidly respond to people's needs. An important example of St. Francis' liberating expression of religious life was a decreasing stress on the mandatory ascetical practices of other religious institutes, such as fasting, making the recitation of the monastic office more essential than ministerial service, stability of location, and so forth. He was undoubtedly harsh with himself—he apologized to Brother Ass before he died, but he imposed fewer demands than the founders before him. Certain fasts he legislated for the brothers when they were at home, but on the road they were to eat what was set before them, as Christ the Lord told the Apostles to do when they were distressed over possible ritual impurities in the preparation of food. Thus St. Francis *related asceticism to charism;* it served the charism. The supreme asceticism was self-denial through self-giving.

All of the components mentioned so far can be applied to many merely natural ventures. Therapists, teachers, statesmen, research scientists, artists, and others must possess freedom of expression, transparency to others affected by their mission, mobility, and optimism. But for a charism to be supernatural, it must have the approval of the believing community. To be "official," the charism must have the *approval of the hierarchy.* As the previous chapter pointed out, St. Francis was not hostile to authority; he did not have to rebel to show that he was different. But he was careful not to seek official sanction of his life style until he was himself assured of its viability.

St. Francis therefore decided to take his band to see Pope Innocent III, who is reputed to have been the strongest personality among the popes of the Middle Ages. It was likely that he was suspicious of any wandering band of men claiming to live the Gospel life, because several groups had already upset the populace in France and the Low Countries by attacking abuses in the Church while they themselves were attempting to live the evangelical life of poverty. St. Francis could not have been unaware of the fracas in the Transalpine Church. "Brothers, I see that the merciful Lord intends to increase our numbers. Let us approach the holy Roman Church, our mother, and make the Pope aware of what the Lord has begun to accomplish by us, in order that we may continue with his good will and directives" (*Legend of the Three Companions*). Thus the liaison with the hierarchy, begun under the aegis of Guido Secondi, Bishop of Assisi, was carried to the Vicar of Christ.

St. Francis at this time was satisfied with verbal approval. We may attribute this attitude to his simplicity and optimism, or to his uncertainty about how long his band would remain together. Because an event of this kind occurred in the dim and hallowed past in a so-called "age of faith," it was not less subject to criticism and doubt, particularly from the participants. To rebuild a few churches is not the same thing as taking seriously the divine mandate to preach the Gospel to every creature. In any case the group was tonsured as a sign of affiliation to the Church and returned to Rivo Torto for two years. This was the first fixed abode of the order, but it was abandoned when the local herdsmen complained that the friars arrogated a hut long in use by themselves. Subsequently St. Francis made the Chapel of Mary in the valley, called the Portiuncula, the center of his activities and the abode to which his heart ever turned.

The bishops, however, were standoffish about the patched friars who invaded their bailiwicks. The saint ultimately realized that the transparency of their personal lives was not enough to win over the clergy. After all, his was a lay movement, without professional theologians—there was only one priest, Sylvester, in the original group. Orthodoxy must always be one of the chief concerns of the hierarchy. But if the Pope himself granted a bull of approval, the bishops would not feel so uneasy. "Under the Church's supervision," as a reliable biographer of St. Francis puts the words into the saint's mouth, "the holy observance of evangelical purity will continuously flower. She will not allow the fragrance of our life to vanish for a single moment" (Celano, *Second Life*).

At the beginning of both *Rules* St. Francis legislates loyalty to the Church. No one may be received contrary to the form and custom of the holy Church. In Chapter Nineteen of the *First Rule* he writes, "All the brothers must be Catholics, and act and speak in the Catholic manner. If anyone should separate from the Catholic faith and way of life in word or in deed and refuse to amend, he shall be expelled from our fraternity." To reinforce the link with the Church he mentions in the *Second Rule* that the brothers are bound to request a Cardinal of the holy Roman Church as governor, protector, and monitor of the order.

If St. Francis had had his way, he would have refused any documents that might have been given him to prevent criticism or persecution of his nascent order. He consistently warned his brothers against seeking written privileges and censured those who had done so during his absence in the Holy Land. He felt that the word of the Supreme Pontiff sufficed, for example, to be the guarantee for the plenary indulgence of the Portiuncula, which was remarkable for its time. In his *Second Rule*, he is adamant in forbidding the brothers to preach in any diocese where the bishop has not given them leave. "My proposal is to soften the heart of prelates through holy humility and respect. Then their invitation to preach will carry greater weight than documents" (*Mirror of Perfection*). Nor would the saint accept gifts of land and plan a friary without the same personally granted permission. As a whole, St. Francis was characterized by unswerving reverence for the clergy. He returns to this theme often in his writings. "We have been given to the clergy as helpers for the salvation of souls. The needs that they are unable to satisfy should be supplied by us" (Celano, *Second Life*). It was precisely because they preached the word of God and confected the Body of Christ that they have a title to the reverence of a Franciscan. "The Lord gave and continues to give me trust in priests who live according to the pattern of the holy Roman Church. . . . I refuse to look for sin in them, because I see the Son of God in them, and thus they are my lords" (*Testament*).

Religious are not bound to a particular prelate once they have received papal approval, it is true. They belong to the hierarchy in its totality as focused in the Holy Father. The division of the Church into dioceses is a human administrative decision. Therefore, although a religious institute needs episcopal approval to function locally, the Vatican II documents are clear in prohibiting bishops from controlling the expression of a religious charism (*Christus Dominus*, 33, and *Perfectae Caritatis*, 8-10). Nevertheless, in the light of St. Francis' own charism, Franciscans of every kind (unlike members of an eremitical order, for example) are to assist the presbyterate of the diocese in their functions, but according to the charism we are attempting to define in these pages. Further, if Franciscans today were to reassess their current position in every diocese and—bypassing all their well-documented privileges—ask the bishop whether they should remain at their posts, change their roles, or surrender their apostolates, they would display the kind of dependence on the good will of the hierarchy that St. Francis considered essential to keep his brothers loyal to the Church. Thus Franciscans would prove their mobility also. They could not allow themselves to become attached to fixed abodes. It is not as if there were other areas of a nation or of the world lacking in which to serve. Perhaps this concept would force religious to "put their best foot forward" at all times. Houses of formation, recuperation, retirement, and so forth would not be included in the frequent reassessment by ecclesiastical superiors, of course, inasmuch as they do not essentially, but only accidentally, serve a ministerial function in a diocese.

Out of the freedom, mobility, and loyalty to the Church grows another dimension of the Franciscan charism, that is, *secularity*. This is made out to be a pejorative term in some quarters. But its denotation is "involved with the world." In contrast with the major trends among religious institutes prior to St. Francis, he thrust his men into the world's pursuits. They were to implement the religious aspect in business, art, government, the military, rural life. This was not to despiritualize the friars' lives. St. Francis preached to the Sultan and his court, noblemen and knights, popes and cardinals, businessmen and farmers. Even more fundamentally, as Pope Benedict XV proclaimed, he made *religious life common property* as a project of his secularity. Tertiaries, who at one time even professed religious vows and wore a distinctive garb, were active in all departments of human endeavor. (A whole chapter of this book—pp. 72-79—is devoted to the secularity of the Franciscan charism.) Because such involvement has been common for centuries of religious life, the innovation of St. Francis is not so apparent to the modern observer.

Monks who lived a life of relative sequestration could not very well present the image of Christ in his full public life—praying in solitude, preaching, training followers to succeed him, laying down his life for others. St. Francis proposed to verify his charism in a *life style as literally close to Christ as possible.* This *emphasis on the humanity of Christ* represented a change in the public and private life of the Church before his time. The joyful glorification of Christ and awareness of his immanence, which was true in the Apostolic Age of the Church in particular, when the memory of the Lord was most vivid, ceded after the time of Constantine to an emphasis on the unapproachable dignity of the God-Man. The awesome majesty of God was implemented by the complex ceremonials surrounding the person of an Oriental emperor of Persia or Byzantium. The action of the Mass was hidden by the iconostasis to remind the worshiper of the gulf between the mystery of God and the lowliness of man.

St. Francis, on the other hand, distilled the joy of living from the Gospels, the Acts, and the Pauline Letters, which continually convey greetings of joy and peace. Our saint's emphasis on the humanity of Christ was coupled with and based upon the Bible. His random opening of the book of the Gospels, the statements of his biographers make clear his reliance on the word of God. Also, for example, there are twelve sentences in Chapter Eleven of the *First Rule;* in them appear fifteen quotations and paraphrases from the Scriptures. "I want my brothers to study the Gospels and progress in truthful knowledge in such a way as to advance at the same time in pure simplicity. Thus they shall not divorce the dove's simplicity from the serpent's wisdom, inasmuch as our good Master joined them in his holy statements" (St. Bonaventure, *Major Legend*).

Lex orandi, lex credendi says the ecclesiastical aphorism: your prayers reflect your beliefs. St. Francis' identification with Christ in his life style brought new theological concepts into doctrinal statements as well as to popular and liturgical prayer forms. We remember how he set up the first crèche at Greccio, Italy, at Christmastime—his favorite of all feasts. One of the great thrills of his mortal life was to travel to the Holy Land (under the safe conduct of the Sultan, whom he had astounded by his simple faith) and walk the earth sanctified by the feet of our Lord. The sacramental presence of Christ in the Eucharist was central to the prayer life of St. Francis, for it was the nearest a man could get on earth to the total person of Christ. This intimate involvement with his brother, Christ, occasioned the sealing of his flesh with the very wounds borne by Christ. Even if one were to reject the supernatural origin of the stigmata—if it were in the natural order—it might bespeak a more remarkable phenomenon in that St. Francis made this identification by sheer force of his will and the sum of his experiences and reflections, rather than that it was caused by the divine intervention. God is also the master of nature; his grace can just as effectively join man's natural process of symbolization without altering physical laws.

Although this crucifixion was not without its physical pains, as witnesses to his life attested, God answered the petition of the saint to feel Christ's anguish even more fully. The order he had founded—almost unwillingly—became so complex, needed such administrative acumen, and to such a degree lost individual contact with him on an intimate level, that he was torn by its loss of mobility and the family spirit. Before the Chapter on May 14, 1217, at the Portiuncula, he verbalized his fear that his very naïveté and lack of learning might put off the educated brothers who had been received into the order. Although the contrary occurred on this occasion, the next decade saw the administrative leadership of the community slip from Francis' hands. His own confreres did reject him, save as a figurehead. "Since my brothers recognize what they are to accomplish and what to avoid (without me), there is nothing left for me to do but teach them by my example. That is why I have been given to them during life and after death" (*Mirror of Perfection*). Although the saint excused himself from governing because of ill health, there are the graver reasons that he finally refused to argue with lax brothers and that he saw the community evolving a charismatic pattern that was inspired by his own, yet differing from it.

Ultimately the testimonial to happiness from identifying with the Crucified is the *perfect joy* of St. Francis. The well-known story is not a theoretical proposition of St. Francis; once more he had the knowledge of experience. The source is the prejudicial *Little Flowers*, but the story line is definitely St. Francis. When Brother Leo asked what perfect joy might be for a Franciscan, the saint replied that it was not in the power to cure and raise the dead, as Christ did; not in knowing all things, including the future and men's hearts, as Christ did; not in the ability to convert all men to God, as Christ did. But if they were standing in the freezing rain, hungry and dirty, at the door of the Portiuncula, and the doorkeeper were to deny them entrance, use abusive language, call them thieves in disguise, and beat them with a stick—"and if we bear all this patiently, keeping in mind the sufferings of Christ, who is worthy of all praise, and how much we should bear out of love for him, Brother Leo, then remember, this is perfect joy!" In the life of St. Francis we see no "credibility gap" between his assertions and his experiences.

A final dimension of the personal charism of our saint must be mentioned before a résumé of all the qualities can be integrated into a single definition. We see in St. Francis a *predilection for the disadvantaged and suffering.* This was not only a humanitarian service—although it was also that. Although humanity is perfectible, the most optimistic person could see that the poor and lepers, for example, had a greater need of spiritual help precisely because the drudgery of physical survival left little time for reflective prayer and diminished belief that God cared for them. Isaiah the prophet made the proclamation of the Good News to poor people one of the signs of the Messiah. If it is true that every Christian shares in the mystery of Christ on earth, then the disadvantaged share especially in Christ's suffering and abandonment.

As Christ had wealthy and influential friends on earth, Joseph of Arimathea, Nicodemus, Mary, Martha, and Lazarus, St. Francis had his Count Orlando, Giacoma de Settesoli, Cardinal Hugolino, and others. Nevertheless he called his brothers the *minores,* the "unimportant." Alert to the needs of the poor, however, St. Francis forbade his brothers to beg at the "table of the Lord" (contrary to popular opinion), unless the labor of their own hands failed to support them. Thus they were not to be parasites in society, but, like St. Paul, join their crafts to their apostolate. Nor would the indigent be deprived of success in their begging. (The chapter on poverty—pp. 95-102—treats this more fully.) *Poverty* is a consequence of assuming the apostolic life and is a practical demand of preaching to the poor—once more—without a "credibility gap." In Chapter Nine of the *First Rule*, St. Francis exhorts the brothers to converse with lowly and despised persons, with the poor and weak, with the sick and lepers, and with beggars in the streets. They were to beg alms as a way of assuming the life of Christ, his mother, and the Apostles.

In summary, we see the personality of a man who grew up into a responsive, flexible, self-confident person, able to take risks. This was the *man* Francis. He had a spiritually based optimism about man's potential to become God's son. His freedom in expressing himself in religious matters was coupled with a willingness to be transparent to others in the process. He attempted to copy the visible ministry of Christ and his Apostles—a leader of a small, mobile band of men, with lives uncluttered by bureaucracy and a multiplicity of regulations. Asceticism was not assumed for its own sake, but only as a consequence of the apostolate and as an imitation of what Christ did. His loyalty to the institutional Church was complete; his adherence to its doctrines was unswerving. But he had no desire to stand outside the pale of the profane world; for him the world was naturally sacred, and the secular and sacred worlds had to become coterminous. Thus, while he assumed a life style as utterly like Christ's as possible, he tried to extend what was originally a lay movement to include even married persons and those unable to copy the itinerant way of Jesus. Whatever deepened his likeness to the human Christ, including physical and mental anguish, contributed to his perfect joy. His mission as an "unimportant brother" of men was especially to the disadvantaged and the poor. This was the *saint and founder*, Francis.

All these factors can now be examined for their common denominator. Life style and spiritually based personality can be fused into a single charismatic concept. Only then what is the enduring legacy to his religious institute can be interpreted existentially according to the common experiences of its members. As the founder expressed it, "O Lord, in this final era of the world, mindful of your ancient loving-kindness, you have established this order of brothers to give stability to your faith and to perfect the mystery of the Gospel through them" (Celano, *Second Life*).

Chapter VI

THE FRANCISCAN CHARISM

IF THE FRANCISCAN CHARISM seems so vague, we can adduce several reasons for it. Our charism is not linked to a particular apostolate: our order is more "representational" than "functional." We are geared to "becoming" more than to "producing." When the "process" of ministry overrides the "person" who is ministering, then our charism becomes less credible. These distinctions are more or less true of all religious, of course. But the distinctions must be kept in mind, because St. Francis, unlike most leaders of men in history, did not dwarf his followers by his overwhelming presence. He helped them to grow taller by his creative approach to religious life. Hence the Franciscan charism tends to assume the face of the one who possesses it. (And Franciscans like to think that, even when historical events ossified the life style of the order, they remained uncategorized as individuals—thanks to the liberating spirit of St. Francis.)

There are several other reasons why the Franciscan charism appears so nebulous. There are so many species and subdivisions of Franciscanism, particularly among the sisterhoods, that they tend to obscure the general pattern in which we should commonly live. Also, many founders after St. Francis incorporated into their movements some of the innovations mentioned in the previous chapter; thus the special Franciscan character of the innovations was lost. Then again, even within the same branch of the order, individual provinces, because of their unique development or apostolate, put a special cast on our common charism as their

51

particular spirit. But the national origin of a province and its orientation to missions or teaching or parochial work need not submerge the basic Franciscan self-concept. A final point concerning the indecision with which we view our own corporate personality is that there is just one spirituality—putting on Christ, who called himself the way, the truth, and our life. All charisms are to be subsumed under the basic Christian struggle to make Christ present to the Church and to the world.

Perhaps the main obstacle to defining the Franciscan charism in the past was that it was narrowly confined to the First Order, rather than to what St. Francis was attempting to accomplish within the whole Church. The definition must apply to both sexes and include the lay tertiaries. Thus we propose here that *the Franciscan charism is to demonstrate that the life of preaching and service led by Christ, his Apostles, and the disciples in first-century Palestine can be successfully lived, even in its externals, in any century and locale.* "Preaching" is not to be understood in the narrow, formal sense, and "service" is broader than the active life. Every phrase in the definition, including the distinction made between Apostles and disciples, has significance. Another way to express the Franciscan charism more succinctly is that *it is our mandate to recall men to the Apostolic Age of the Church.* After St. Francis left the scene of his work upon his death, he still lingered on by the force of his personality. It goes without saying, of course, that it was the Holy Spirit who guided the first disciples of St. Francis. The existence of opposing ideas among equally sincere followers of Francis in succeeding centuries is another instance of the polarization mentioned earlier in this book.

The Franciscan Order, we then see, is in its threefold dimension to replicate the experiences of the Apostles, who in turn consecrated other men for the task of establishing communities of Christians. In these earliest communities we read also of the holy women dedicated to the service of the faithful and of the world at large. We can find further analogies, such as that between secular tertiaries and those first apostolic foundations which were most responsive to the teaching of Christ, even to the point of "sharing everything in common" (cf. Acts 2:44). This recall to the Apostolic Age is our "theological model" or the framework of our ministerial labor. Here, once more "ministry" refers both to the lay and to the priestly state, and to both men and women. The prophetic role of St. Francis was precisely to give voice to this earlier variety of expression in religion, the former mobility of mission, the concern of primitive Christians to rise from their Eucharistic agape and serve the disadvantaged, and their joyful involvement with the secular world. Above all, St. Francis gave voice and meaning to the vivid memory of the human Christ as if he had ascended into heaven just yesterday. As Pope Benedict XV remarked, "St. Francis made religious life common property." This quotation can be restated that evangelical poverty, chastity, and obedience are possible to priest, Brother, Sister, married or unmarried lay person.

Every component of the Franciscan charism must be related to the individual's perception of himself somehow serving—"I am in your midst as the one who serves you"—and somehow preaching—"faith comes through hearing." The question arises why St. Francis, who is supposed to be a kind of guidepost or novicemaster even today, was so adamant in enforcing certain Gospel insights. A guidepost, of course, has to convey its meaning adequately. Hence, as was said above, after our saint returned from the Holy Land to Italy in the spring of 1220 or 1221, he repudiated such changes in his charism as large and permanent establishments, monastic observances, and difficult fasts inconsistent with almsgathering and traveling. He was especially unhappy with written privileges that led to pretentiousness and induced a certain laxity, because the brothers were under less constraint to give the more important documentation of their lives well lived. The brothers should not have whereon to lay their heads, he said. Fasting was the privilege of imitating Christ in his forty-day abnegation, but should not become a regulation for its own sake. Therefore every aspect of the brothers' lives began by a comparison with the statement of Scriptures. We hear St. Francis say (in words whose viewpoint was later echoed by St. Vincent de Paul addressing the Daughters of Charity): "Wherever we move, we keep our cell with us. Brother Body is our cell. The hermit who dwells inside is our soul, keeping contact with God and meditating upon him. In fact, if the soul does not stay at home in reflection, any cell made by hands is useless for a religious" (*Mirror of Perfection*).

Because charism is subject to hierarchy, if it is to achieve an "official" status, religious need formal and precise instruction in the charism. This is to be given within an ideal community. A house of formation is the place where the person spontaneously discovers how he or she can be set free to love others, meanwhile "practicing" this concept and testing it under the supervision of persons well suited to provide these experiences. But even in houses of training, the life style must include *service* to others inside and outside the immediate community and *preaching*, not just by example, but also by "exhorting one another" and "confessing their sins to one another," and by "joyful songs and spiritual canticles," as we read of the primitive Church in the New Testament. The community must be small enough for a continual face-to-face charity with every other member. Thus each member learns to become transparent to the rest; no one should be able to "escape" into anonymity and facelessness.

Each community of Franciscans should follow the theological model of the Apostles and the disciples. The disciples were those persons who were not mobile, but stayed at home as part of the local community formed by a spiritual leader. Like today's secular tertiaries, they had family commitments or were simply unequal to the active life. On the other hand, modern active religious and priests look to the Apostles, who shared the experiences of close living, were sent into specific locales to bring the good news, and then returned to be strengthened in conviction and take consolation from their loving community. St. Francis represents the attempt to restore these ideas to the world. If our own time does see a rebirth of this creative expression of religious life, we will immediately have to resist ossification and permanent structuring, of course. To keep the charism alive in the Church, the authority should dismiss a candidate who does not give ample promise of preaching and serving and living in a community of lovers. Incidentally, the small, experimental communities we see rising all over the Catholic world seem to be a recovery of some of the ideas brought out in these pages to explain the Franciscan charism. But if the experiment is merely humanitarian social service, or if the members do not regularly pray, eat, and relax together, then the life style of Christ with the Apostles (or the Apostles with their constituents) is not convalidated.

Truthfully, it was easier for St. Francis to imitate the life style of the first century during the thirteenth century than it is for us. There is a greater likeness between the first and thirteenth centuries than between our lives and those of just one hundred years ago—in food eaten, fabrics worn, the recreation possible, the careers available, the science known, the philosophy taught. Life for the earlier centuries was geared to the flocks and to the soil, with some merchandising in the larger towns and seaports. Nowadays swift travel, communications media, and technological aids have expanded not only the means of spreading the good news, but also of spreading its competition. It is not so clear in our day what is useful, but not luxurious, what is supportive of nature, but not indulgence. Since Christ or Francis could not have established a precedent, modern Franciscans have to solve the problem—and generally it will be on the individual rather than on the collective level, as is fitting in an order where individual expression is valued. (The role of the superior will be to keep the aspiration level high.) The existing and past *Rules* of tertiaries forbade them vanity in dress, for example. Now a lay woman must decide what clothes are vanity for a tertiary, and a religious Sister what hair style (for the unveiled) shows preoccupation, as St. Paul warned!

An example of how a charism continues to evolve in its details according to the perceptions of its members and even of its founder can be seen in some passages of the *Rule* of the First Order. St. Francis seems to be more severe than the Gospel itself, but certainly not holier than Christ. He forbids his brothers to receive coins or money for their labor, allowing only food or goods for their needs. Yet Christ had a treasurer and paid the coin of the tribute; obviously he accepted money. It was only for their missionary journeys, as we read in the sixth chapter of St. Mark (vv. 7 ff.) and in similar passages, that Christ gave a prohibition against receiving coins, for reasons we shall explain. In this chapter of St. Mark we see how Christ toured the villages of Galilee, then sent his Apostles in pairs as a follow-up. They were allowed a staff, but no food, money, or "suitcase." They could have sandals, but no extra tunics. They were to stay in the same house, once they were established in a locality, lest they appear to be unstable or seeking the best accommodations. St. Luke and St. Matthew record Christ as allowing no staff; the point is trivial, but the sense is apparent: simplicity and detachment. The historical point is that Christ did not want his Apostles' public image to be less than that of the itinerant rabbis of the day, who lived by donations and the overnight hospitality of the local people. The Apostles probably left their gear with Christ, to whom they had to return to make their report. In any case, one must recover the sense of Scriptures rather than slavishly imitate the externals of St. Francis' life. Every Franciscan must continue to read the Gospels, Acts, and Epistles to garner insights about life style. Historical criticism and comparative literature teach us more precisely about the meaning of the Scriptures on which we found our lives—just as the behavioral sciences help us to achieve personhood.

Later in the passage cited from St. Mark, after the missions of the Apostles were completed, Christ tells them to repair to a secluded place and refresh themselves—just as members of a religious institute theoretically return to a place of relaxation and mutual love after their daily exertions. Yet when the people discovered what they were going to do, Christ relented and began to teach again, because the people were "like untended sheep" (verse 34). Accessibility to the needy or apostolic availability is the touchstone of the Franciscan life, turning daily chores in an office, kitchen, classroom, or pulpit into an occasion of preaching and serving. In that same passage from St. Mark, Christ is seen feeding the multitude miraculously in promise of the Eucharist. We see him continuously supplying both the temporal and spiritual needs of those "untended sheep."

We see the same accessibility or availability in the life of the early Franciscans. Even when St. Francis retired from superiorship and was debilitated in health, he said, "I believe it pleases God more for me to interrupt my retirement and pursue my labors" (St. Bonaventure, *Major Legend*). As Christ and the Apostles were preaching primarily to possessors of the true revelation of God, the Jews, with a few forays among the Samaritans and the Gentiles of the Decapolis, so St. Francis and his first followers were sent primarily to believers. Yet he was the first religious founder who included a Chapter in his *Rule* about missions to the Saracens and other non-believers. We perhaps can say that St. Francis was attempting to establish ideal communities of lovers at every level of society—priestly, religious, and lay. He hoped to convert bishops and priests to the fullness of evangelical life as Christ hoped to convert the Scribes, Pharisees, and Sanhedrin to the fullness of the divine revelation. In the first, thirteenth, or twentieth century, adults brought up in the true faith are not necessarily committed to living it when the crisis of change is presented to them.

Apparently, in the mind of St. Francis the apostolic life (which is a narrower concept than the "Gospel life," if we examine the terms) did not necessarily or even typically include formal, pulpit preaching, but rather manual labor, good example, and simple exhortation. "The minister should not grant permission to preach to everyone indiscriminately. In any case, all the brothers should preach by their works" (*First Rule*, Chapter Seventeen). St. Francis has St. Paul, the tentmaker, in mind. He tells the brothers to support themselves by manual labor, not in authoritative positions as chamberlains, cellarers, and overseers; they are to remain inferior to all in the household. Although the founder makes the canonical distinction of his brothers into "clerics" and "laics" in Chapter Seventeen, as well as in the *Second Rule* and *Testament*, in Chapter Twenty-One of the *First Rule* he permits all the brothers to give words of exhortation to men and praise to God—of which he immediately subjoins an example. Because of Chapter Nine of the *Second Rule* legislating about the examination and approval of preachers, we can infer that this is once more a reference to pulpit preaching by a priest trained in theology—or at least a "cleric," that is, a deacon, as St. Francis was himself.

We are astonished to read that, by the time of the sixth general, St. Bonaventure, it was forbidden to receive brothers into the order to be used as domestics in the household, unless the minister general himself allowed it. It was not merely a question of appearing to have servants. St. Bonaventure wished to maintain the status of a clerical order, trained in theology, so the heretical element of some uneducated brothers, which plagued him during his whole generalate, might not rise again. Thus the idea of St. Francis that the unlearned "lay" member of his order could preach by simple exhortation was lost as part of the charismatic expression of the primitive age of the Friars Minor.

There can be no doubt that such preaching can be made by Sisters, and by men and women tertiaries within the context of their daily business—that is, if they have the courage to join words to the preaching of good example and service. Truly the teaching of Christian doctrine—which does require training, of course—is a marvelous opportunity to give the exhortation which is so Franciscan. At least "secular" tertiaries at their meetings and "regular" tertiaries (religious Brothers and Sisters) should deliver public words of exhortation to one another as a matter of course.

Chapter VII

THE COMMON LIFE AND INDIVIDUATION

To BELONG TO A COMMUNITY of worshipers is part of the Christian life. The "common life," as the phrase is used here, refers to the familial arrangements of most religious *institutes*. But the religious *state*, as it was defined in preceding chapters, does not require the common life by its nature—although throughout history that is how most institutes evolved. In the light of the broad definition of the Franciscan charism given above, we recall that in both the age of the Apostles and the age of St. Francis the common life in some sense was typical.

Some groups of the early Christians "shared everything in common" (Acts 2:44). They were pledged to show charity above all "to the household of the faith" (Gal. 6:10). The secular tertiary groups analogously are to have a common fund, common prayer life, and an apostolate peculiar to each fraternity, shared in by all. At one time the intensification of baptismal vows included the pronouncing of religious vows by tertiaries living with their families outside the cloister. They even wore distinctive garb prescribed by their laws. As "secular" tertiaries they were completely involved in the world. To underscore their family orientation, St. Francis originally called them the Brothers and Sisters of Penance. As these remarks are implemented in the chapter on Franciscan "secularity" (pp. 72-79), we can confine ourselves here to discussion of "regular" Franciscans of the Three Orders.

St. Francis backed away from the earlier forms of religious community. St. Augustine's community of priests was a professional group, tied, as it were, to the ministry of the altar. St. Benedict gave individual monasteries much freedom and autonomy to adapt locally, but to Francis they were too large, stationary, and seemingly only parallel to the world, rather than involved in it. Missionary monks were more to the taste of St. Francis, but they, too, desired mostly to reduplicate their monastic life in another land. The Cluniac reform was based on the kind of community exemption from bishops eschewed by St. Francis, and was geared to the clerical and scholarly life. St. Robert of Molesme, who founded Citeaux, introduced more poverty and made of his foundation a lay movement; but once more St. Francis was not drawn to the large numbers and isolation. In short, our saint wanted smaller, mobile groups, who were loosely attached to a base of operations.

The life of the Apostles was loosely structured. Their "home" was any "base of operations" that was a haven of spiritual fellowship and physical refreshment—a springboard back into full engagement with the world. Regarding the First Order, the very word "friar" means "brother." St. Francis envisioned such families as the pattern of his foundation. The superior was to be the first among equals. "I want my brothers to consider themselves the sons of the same mother," he said. "If anyone requires a tunic, a cord, or anything else, another brother should give it to him gladly. . . . Indeed, he should practically force him to take it" (Celano, *Second Life*). In both of his *Rules*, St. Francis goes beyond brotherhood and tells his followers to make known their needs to one another, cherishing each other as a mother might provide for a child. They are even to wash each other's feet (*First Rule*, Chapter Six). When the natural mother of a certain brother was in need, St. Francis sold a copy of the Scriptures to help "our mother," because he felt a special relationship to her through his confrere.

Religious institutes, however they may structure themselves—a community of hermits, monks, friars, secular tertiaries, cloistered nuns, or active Sisters—are meant to be a model, the "city on a hill," to which the Church and the world can look for an example of love and productive cooperation. More than the blood-related family, a religious family has members who are resource persons to each other on an equal footing. Subordination is not to be based on the factor of age, but on the greater need to be directed by a person of greater skill—in liturgy, spiritual growth, professional competence, the community's goals as a group. One supposes that the religious family has a greater compatibility because of the members' common objectives and life style, plus the accumulated ongoing experience of many generations.

There are obvious spiritual advantages in living the common life. It provides a check on whether one is acting merely to satisfy his own ego needs through some "private" apostolate or is sincerely serving the needs of the Church. Moreover, a worthwhile venture would cease in the event of the originator's death or poor health, or on account of the lack of helpers, unless there is a community to support the project. A member of an institute with a ministry achieved by the common life (unlike most "freelance" religious) can make his full-time witness explicit. The "isolate" religious must be occupied in making a living, to which the free service of others must be subordinated. The religious identifiable as members of an institute (a special "habit" is not crucial here) should be able to manifest more clearly the glory of the eschatological Church, a community perfected in love. Such persons are, finally, granted access to many more places and persons than are denied them by reason of their obvious institutional membership.

It seems evident that one could carry the notion of a friary or convent as a family too far with respect to parental authority. For Franciscans the local community is like a *family* insofar as it shares a common home and table. The attitude of commonality this engenders does not alter the fact that members of a family have diverse careers and personal fulfillments that can carry them far from their home most of the day. In the religious family, too, a variety of personal endeavors does not necessarily destroy the family attitude.

Further, the local community is like a *brotherhood* insofar as authority arises from within itself, not paternalistically. Although the order began with a patriarchal government, even in the founder's lifetime it passed to a senatorial, partly representative type of rule. The word "brotherhood" likewise suggests a relationship qualified by a common spiritual ancestry and a corporate destiny.

Finally, the local community is like a *democracy* insofar as its leadership, once conferred by the consent of the governed, is exercised through regular (constitutional) channels. The basis of leadership is support of the group's charism in the Church. Family, brotherhood, and democracy are viable only in proportion to the degree of interpersonal communication and transparency so prized by St. Francis. It is interesting to recall in the context of the last two paragraphs on the common life and the local community an anecdote in the life of St. Francis. In 1209 St. Francis was about to take his small band, under the patronage of Cardinal John Colonna, to see Pope Innocent III. They elected Bernard of Quintavalle, not St. Francis, to lead them. In their democratic family they recognized the superior skills of this knowledgeable brother—whence flowed his obvious leadership in a venture to achieve the next step in validating their charism, that is, hierarchical approval. Thus Bernard played Aaron to the Moses of St. Francis.

Family, brotherhood (or sisterhood), and democracy—these are some dimensions of Franciscan community life. But how are these dimensions retained in a practical way? There is no single formula, of course, but in every social group some criteria need to be maintained to reinforce the common life as far as it is applicable to individual situations. To reduce common life to a mere mental attitude is farcical; without concrete acts as the sign of this attitude, common life begins to fail.

Christ sent his Apostles forth "two by two"—but from some base of operations, to which they returned to make their reports to him. Similarly, St. Francis sent his brothers forth from the friary "like pilgrims and strangers in the world" (*First Rule,* Chapter Six), to work with their hands, to seek alms, to preach with simple exhortation. The friary was a springboard into secular society; to the friary they returned for rest and spiritual refreshment. Their state was obviously fluid, but the thrust of their lives was to hurry back to their communities. It is this allegiance that is the final support of home life, fraternity, and democracy. Those who are without such allegiance are using the friary or convent for a hotel.

It is not that a totally simultaneous life is the important thing, nor should one wish to be immersed into a super-sized community. Number, of course, is related to compatibility of the members and the apostolates of the community. If we trust the Vatican II documents (*Decree on the Ministry and Life of Priests*), then the Eucharistic celebration is the source and root of community life for every Christian group. The point here is to be realistic without, on the other hand, totally canceling the common prayer life. One meal a day toward evening, shared in relaxation with our co-religious and cronies, is the social reinforcement of what occurs at Mass. A typical day should include these three elements to some minimal degree: the Eucharist, a common meal, and spontaneous recreation.

Obviously there are even long periods when individual members are off on business or holiday; this fact does not preclude the common life. But the frame of reference of our activities is the ideal community into which we draw the less outgoing members and give evidence of transparency to them ourselves. No community survives unless the members are accessible to each other's needs and actually communicate—not just pretend. Without some common "exercises" there is simply no possibility for encounter with the group as a group—it would be like belonging to a union and never attending meetings, socials, or voting.

A religious community exists for the Church's mission, but it also presents itself to the world in a way that benefits the members. One practical spiritual application in St. Francis' mind is that the first apostolate of the community is to itself. Members sanctify one another by their helpfulness. Christ's primary activity in his public life was to sanctify and form his Apostles into a believing and worshiping community by example and correction. St. Francis remarked (*First Rule*, Chapter Five) that if a brother lives according to the flesh rather than the spirit, his confreres should humbly, but diligently warn, instruct, and correct the erring brother. In Chapter Seven he goes on to tell his followers to respect and honor each other for a spiritual reason and not to murmur against a confrere.

Let us make a brief application of the statements of the present chapter to a community of eight Franciscan Sisters teaching in a parish school. The large and expensive parish convent would be unnecessary. A modest wage—probably much less than that paid to lay teachers—would support the Sisters' renting of two apartments in the locale of their teaching. St. Francis' dislike of owning property and living pretentiously or apart from people would thus be adequately expressed. Despite the raise in salary, the parish would gain by not having to buy land, build and maintain a convent. Religious would learn the value of money and the need to live like their neighbors. If Franciscan Sisters (one cannot speak for the charism of others) were to gravitate to the parishes with higher standards and salaries, the whole believing community would recognize (and rightly scoff at) their low-grade charism. The Sisters would worship before and after school in the parish church—no insignificant witness in itself. This brand of common life and mobile structure applies as readily to nursing and social-service Sisters. Meanwhile the major superior would visit the Sisters often to support their ventures and see to their needs. (Houses of formation are considered separately below, pp. 66-70.)

The result of the free-wheeling behavior of St. Francis is that our order fosters a spirit of greater spontaneity than many other institutes, but this fact is not always apparent in Franciscan history. Nevertheless, the complexities of ancient restrictions never quite destroyed the idea that "Franciscan" suggests informality, hospitality, good cheer, and the family spirit. The absence of regimentation and, ideally, the accessibility of superiors should permit the individuality of a Franciscan to increase. The hallmark of the Franciscan is to be a *bon vivant* in the religious sense and within the framework of the vows, without becoming an "oddball."

As St. Paul described it, we ought to have the "glorious freedom of the children of God" (Rom. 8:21). This excludes the notion of living under a tyrant. It bespeaks a sense of filiation and family spirit with God, not with men alone. But freedom by itself has a negative description; it is the "absence of some restriction." St. Paul's idea is positive; law is *internalized and self-imposed.* No religious is ever free to be the unique individual God calls him to become, until he no longer *needs* prohibitions laid upon him. The paradox of Christianity is that only the unfree person needs the burden of law. Hence the writer of the Epistle says that those who had lived under the law of Moses had a heavy burden, but by their adoption into God's family as Christians they become free by reason of their love-relationship, which is the primary "command" of the New Testament.

The internalization of law is never likely to occur if it does not happen in the houses of formation. There is seldom much similarity between them and "real-life" houses, however. Houses of formation should be small enough to prevent any candidate's submersion in numbers. They are no place to send senior members who are disturbed by and critical of the apparently erratic behavior of the young. They should not be made a refuge for derelicts, penitents, the mentally ill, and those incapable of living peacefully anywhere else. How can an authentic community be built up? Houses of formation do need older members with great flexibility and charity to provide the important example of joyful maturity. In the dreadful and un-Franciscan super-communities of some Sisters—consisting of aspirants, postulants, novices, scholastics, senior Sisters, and what-not—the only way to reconcile the situation is to give each group a sense of identity through the appointment of separate superiors, independence of action, and liturgies to suit the participants— under separate chaplains, if possible. This ideal is often impractical as houses of formation are presently set up, but it should be planned for the future. Most Franciscans will not live in huge houses after formation; hence their training is unrealistic if the Constitutions and lectures present one standard and the apostolate another.

The novitiate is a period of self-analysis and some sequestration, but it cannot be totally unrelated to the apostolate and separate from the other houses of the province. Novices should travel to other houses which are near enough and even remain there a day or two to observe. (This does not violate the integrity of a canonical year if it does not exceed three months[1] in totality.) They should see the alcoholics, the sick, and the "oddballs"— whether they are priests or Brothers or Sisters. The local religious could explain their ministry and answer the frank questions of the young. Thus the principles enunciated in training could be given a more realistic setting.

This last paragraph refers, of course, to a novitiate year which comes prior to wearing the habit and taking first vows. In the institutes which now place the novitiate at the end of the total

---

[1] *Instruction on the Renewal of Religious Formation* (United States Catholic Conference, 1969), pp. 14f.

formation program—for the priest, before he has received major orders; for the Sister, after she has been on mission for a few years—such novices already have been in close contact with other houses of the province. Probably the most desirable time for a person to enter the novitiate is at the point where, after adequate counseling, he himself feels the need to prepare for the total commitment of final vows—whenever that might occur during formation. To avoid caprice and disruption of an apostolate, the candidate could give a year's notice, at which time, however, the major superior might request some compromise for the good of the province.

In Franciscan history it often seemed that the formation process was successful if the individual had reached a total conformity with traditional behavior patterns, particularly those of thought. Now we realize that formation is successful only when the individual emerges enough to support the community charism with his special talents. St. Paul taught us that *every* Christian has a particular gift to offer the community. Celano puts these words in the mouth of St. Francis: "God does not cater to special individuals. The minister general of the order, who is the Holy Spirit, settles upon a poor and simple person as easily as upon another" (Celano, *Second Life*). Counterfeit "gifts" of the Spirit are generally obvious. When one brother was applauded for not breaking silence by even going to confession, St. Francis called it rather a gift of the devil. And when a young brother groaned during his sleep because of hunger pains after excessive fasting, St. Francis wakened him to have a full meal and an object lesson.

The satisfaction of a Franciscan in his ministerial role should not be founded on his environment. Once granted the freedom to do his work reasonably well, the strong religious should *ideally* transcend the onus of the common life, such as irritating personalities, a suspicious superior, minimal living standards, and a lack of time for reflection and relaxation. *Realistically* one's total environment is a conditioner of his role satisfaction. In a house of formation, however, one's self-concept flows almost totally from intra-community factors: recognition by authority, acceptance to the next level of training, emergence of the individual through attempts at self-expression in a non-threatening environment, the perception of growth through learning, and so forth. Because of the only limited apostolate possible to trainees, the "feedback" that is supportive of one's own worth and relevance is derived almost completely from the common life. For this last reason above all, in a house of formation individuation occurs *by means of* the common life.

The training process must allow, even encourage, the deviations from itself that bring about the very goals for which the process exists. Although maximum use of personal talents is desirable, nevertheless, insofar as charism must be guided by authority for the good of the whole group, this use is not always possible in any life, not only religious life. The excruciating frustration of one's *activities* does not necessarily cause the frustration of one's *inner growth*, both psychologically and spiritually. Nevertheless, those persons consistently incapable of such frustration should not remain in religious life. Nor should those who are unfit for the joyful burden of obedience—for grudging obedience is a caricature of religious life. If superiors, on the other hand, habitually "test" subjects or prefer the letter of the law to its spirit during the period of formation, the process of individuation is retarded—possibly even stopped—because the candidate develops a whole set of psychologically crippling responses in order to survive in religious life.

Loyalty to the institute does not necessarily mean conformity. To love the order one should be willing to risk everything, including personal disgrace or crucifixion, to improve it. Religious, insofar as they represent an officially sanctioned modality of the Gospel life, should be freed to become what nature and grace have indicated. Education and formation should be flexible enough to give the young religious the conviction that he is trusted—and is mature enough to develop within the greater context of the Franciscan charism. Candidates generally enter religious life with a docile spirit; they are eager to serve God and man through the institute. They trust the insights of older religious until they "learn" that conformity, mindless obedience, and exterior religiosity seem to be rewarded in their organization. Individuality is called "singularity." Friendship is suspect. Originality is reckoned as divisive. Meanwhile Franciscan optimism and romanticism and freedom of emotional expression are left to the biographies of St. Francis and sermons to the laity.

Age and experience deserve respect, not for their own sake, but because they presume maturity and wisdom apart from the tally of years. The Spirit, however, does not confine himself to age brackets. He speaks to everyone who is willing to listen. An institute or province divided into factions by *aggiornamento* is wasting its time on dialogue and self-study and updating. If the segregation of minds is that complete, with nobody in the middle, the love-relationship which is the pulse of the community is already defunct. If anything destroys individuation, it is having the viewpoint of the stronger imposed on the weaker, regardless of who may finally be proved correct by history.

The customs taught to young religious should not be imposed, but proposed as the typical behavior of seasoned religious. But if there is a double standard, and the older Sisters, Brothers, and priests do not live by the so-called customs and ascetical practices, they were surely unreal in the first place. The style of life of young religious should grow out of observing older religious. Otherwise it would seem that the final results in the conduct of older persons do not justify the training "process" and the multiplicity of regulations.

The individuation of a Franciscan is never complete when he lives a merely useful life. This could be only good citizenship and great humanitarianism. He must have loving sonship and the continuing contact of prayer to live a full life. One does not need a long life to have a full life. To have lived a full life is to have lived long enough. In order to become a fully actualized person with his potentials brought to the surface, one needs the liberating action of sonship and prayer. Personhood is not a static summation of qualities or achievements. Personhood is a dynamic state, characterized by the capacity for *change* (the sign of growth) and *self-expression* (the sign of uniqueness).

St. Francis was such a total person. Therefore, he gave himself to others, expended physical effort to live the apostolic life, even at the cost of his own health, as we recall from his increasing blindness and stomach disease. He communicated his intellectual and emotional life by passionately proposing his innovations and idealism to the scrutiny of the Church and the world. He shared his spiritual life by giving us his prayers, confessing his weaknesses, and bringing us to his awareness of the human Christ. The ability to expose oneself is a sign of maturity, for it subjects the ego to the risk of rejection by others—which often happened to Francis. The strong supernatural faith of St. Francis reinforced his naturally strong ego in the presentation of his charism to other men.

Chapter VIII

FRANCISCAN SECULARITY

WE HAVE CALLED THE FRANCISCAN CHARISM a demonstration that the Gospel life can be successfully lived in any condition or time of life—that is, it is a call given to men and women, married and celibate, priests and laymen to return to the Apostolic Age of the Church. If this be accurate, it follows that all ranks of mankind should be able to see their particular status in life being fulfilled by Franciscans somewhere and their special problems interpreted for them through the evangelical life. For this reason Franciscans do not claim to *do* something special in the Church, but try to *mean* something special. Teachers, office workers, scientists, parish priests, clowns, cloistered women, mothers, and ditch-diggers should be able to look to Franciscans for a model of the Christ-life within the present moment. To fulfill their charism, Franciscans must penetrate all of society. Historically, the three orders have attempted this; they remain the largest group in the Church oriented to a single charism. Their degree of success in restoring the creative age of the Apostles is subject to debate, of course.

In the *Second Rule*, Chapter Six, the founder tells his brothers to be "as pilgrims and strangers in this world, serving the Lord in poverty and humility." This does not sound like world-shaking involvement. But one cannot quote a man outside the context of his actions. (We remember that Christ told us to turn our back on father and mother—cf. Luke 14:26.) St. Francis' movement was "secular" in contrast to the existing religious life.

72

He did not permit his brothers to live an eremitical life. For those who needed periodic sequestration he provided the *retiro*, with a special rule of life, requiring at least four brothers for this community of silence and prayer. Thus he did not believe that the solitary life was for his followers. In the Chapter at Assisi in 1269, St. Bonaventure decreed that hermits were not to make profession in the order. As a matter of fact, the original twelve followers of St. Francis came from many walks of life—lawyer, priest, businessman, soldier, peasant. Having known the world, they were better adapted to transform it.

The profane world can become the sacred world, if men make it so. We see this reflected in the poem of St. Francis, *The Canticle of Brother Sun*, in which he calls the world of nature and even Sister Death to praise the Lord God. Similarly a painter, architect, or plumber who is faithful to the truth within him serves the God of truth in the best religious sense; the "maker" is aware of his limitations, respects the materials in his hand, and completes the work of creation by improving the human milieu.

Before St. Francis, secularity was the less-than-best way to serve God, although there were religious and priests who did live among men. They did not work alongside them, however, as did the original followers of St. Francis and the tertiaries after them. Typically, the religious person found God in a cloister; those who gave witness to the dignity of labor wore a Benedictine habit. Particularly before the great number of priests joined him, St. Francis considered his movement—what was to become the First Order—a layman's recall to the Gospel life. Thus, in the *First Rule*, before he developed his own charism completely, he wrote, "The brothers should occupy themselves in the arts they understand. . . . Each should remain in the skill or craft from which he was called to religious life. . . . And they may keep the tools and instruments necessary for their work" (*First Rule*, Chapter Seven). We remember that, although Christ called a publican and fishermen to leave their occupations, the soldiers and farmers and rich merchants were simply commanded to live justly and in love. St. Francis saw his brothers as the leaven in the lump of dough, mingling with the common folk in their homes and fields and shops. Later, the First Order became specifically apostolic, primarily because the priests, whose "natural" work was preaching, were also to remain in the "craft" from which they had entered the order. One is inclined to think that the founder prescribed in the *Second Rule* that the unlearned brother should not be anxious to acquire learning, in order to retard the clericalization of his order. In any case, it was the Third Order which finally became the lay Franciscan movement.

Cloistered Franciscans, such as the Poor Clares, seem to be an enigma with respect to the charism of our order. In what sense does their community life demonstrate that the evangelical life proposed by Christ in the first century can be successfully lived in any century?

First of all, the cloistered cannot be ignorant of the world's needs—political, social, moral. Their "secularity" or involvement presents a risk to their way of life, but all acts of faith are a risk. The Franciscan cannot be realistically insulated against the world. It may be the charism of a Carmelite nun to sequester herself—she alone can be sure—but not a Franciscan. Involvement means that the Poor Clare monastery should be set in the midst of a city where, like a Christian community of prayer set upon a mountain, everyone, especially the spiritually indigent, can see the life of voluntary poverty, the sharing with the deprived what is given to the convent as alms, and a joyful accessibility for those who come to the parlor.

The disadvantaged, the emotionally disturbed, the despairing should be able to seek out the Clares and also hear a "simple exhortation," receive spiritual comfort, and join in uplifting prayer. The day should come when some Clares are trained in counseling techniques to aid the poor of Christ. That this has not happened in the past is no reason that it cannot happen in the future. This need not make the monastery a clinic, but a refuge for the theologically and emotionally guilty—a place where no barriers of an appointment, a secretary, questionnaires, and testing programs separate a client from a human encounter in the moment of need.

Hopefully, the inhuman custom of the grille will cease in order to permit authentic face-to-face charity. Thus, although the Clares cannot go among the laity, they can live alongside them. They must learn to be secure in the dysfunctionality of their roles in our age, which measures a person's worth by the tangible results of his activity and his ability to compete for the attention of the world. They proclaim the hope of resurrection better by intimacy with God than by any social hyperactivity. Our Clares make the silent, prayerful, and poor Christ present to the Church and to the world. They, too, are women of joy, optimism, free expression, and romantic idealism. When this is not verified in a convent, it is because the leaders do not trust this spontaneity and this openness to the neighborhood of the monastery. Thus the life of the Poor Clare is an adaptation of the Franciscan charism, in which accessibility is still a dimension of the Gospel.

The non-cloistered, active Franciscan Sisters of the various Third Order groups have already been considered in the chapter on community life, particularly with respect to their experimentation and mobility. Just as the Poor Clares were urged to be more accessible to the needy—as, for example, in counseling—tertiary religious ought to seek out the disadvantaged in areas of life where the Gospel has not been adequately demonstrated as the source of religious activity—dope-addiction, suicide-prevention, mental retardation, senescence. Such groups need a nucleus of religious around which to form a "total-life" Christian community, wherein the hope of resurrection assuages human grief. The religious tertiary is given to the world not just to live a parallel life with the needy nor to enter their lives sporadically. She is not bound to the cloister like the Clare, nor to the altar like a priest, nor to a family like most secular tertiaries. She can, therefore, with her co-religious be the magnet to which the needy gravitate for an experience of total Christian life in new institutional forms. These religious should be "secular" enough to prepare professionally and to use government aid to bring dedication to fields where there exists a danger that persons become only "case histories." Of course, they must beware of seeking glamorous and dramatic apostolates for other than spiritual reasons.

The final comments on Franciscan secularity are reserved for the group to which they are eminently applicable—the Third Order Secular, the "lay person" in his home. These men and women are the parade example of Gospel secularity. St. Francis tried not so much to "bring" God to the world as to show that he was already there. In the words of St. Bonaventure, the universe bears the *vestigia*, the "footprints," of God; we must track him down among us, especially in each other. St. Francis neither surrenders to the Secular City nor destroys it; he makes in his Third Order a single habitation for God and man. By improving the world and continuing the work of creation, man sanctifies the universe as his worship of God. But the man who attempts this must first himself be holy and practicing the evangelical counsels. No one can know the Word of God, by whom all things were made and without whom nothing was made, unless the heavenly Father reveals him.

In a sense, the Third Order Secular has represented for seven hundred years a "glorification" of the common man; for he, too, shares in a religious charism and in the religious state. The title of "minors" identifies the First Order members as nonentities in the medieval world; St. Francis even asked Hugolino, the Cardinal Protector, to bring the friars who were seeking preferments and prelacies down to earth (Celano, *Second Life*). The title of "Poor Ladies of St. Damian" originally identified the Second Order as unendowed women living by alms. The Third Order

Secular can add to unglamorous and otherwise pedestrian lives the extra spiritual factor of living in obedience to canonical superiors, without property as a status symbol, and in the chastity of married or single life.

Tertiaries are particularly courteous and cheerful, lest there be some "credibility gap" between their profession and life style. They are devoted to the humanity of God's Son. Their modesty or "continency" in living, homes, clothes, cars, and so forth attests to their following of the poor Christ. They share themselves and their resources (financial, psychological, and spiritual) with others in the fraternity in idealized community life. Optimistically they believe and expect and cause others to rise to a higher level of aspiration. Above all, they have that sense of freedom and transparency of self-expression and joy of life—even in suffering—that is the hallmark of the Franciscan charism. St. Francis' creative approach to religious life permeates their lives as well, so the tertiaries also share in the mandate to return to the Apostolic Age of the Church.

Thus, canonized tertiaries have come from all social categories and careers—royalty and peasants, martyrs and penitents, lawyers and businessmen, physicians and blacksmiths. Several founders and foundresses of other institutes began as tertiaries and crystallized their movement into a religious congregation. The Curé of Ars considered the Third Order the means God intended to elevate parishes morally. King St. Louis of France and Queen St. Elizabeth of Hungary were chosen the chief tertiary patrons, not because of their rank but precisely because, in spite of their rank, they did not idle their lives away uselessly. St. Joan of Arc, a tertiary called by Mark Twain the "genius of disinterested patriotism," became a saint by responding to her inner voices. She was not a martyr to the faith—she was battling another Catholic nation and was condemned by a Church tribunal (or a travesty of one). But she was a "martyr" in the sense of being a "witness"—in her response to the inspiration to unite her nation, which we may call her personal charism. Her austere clothes, hair style, and lack of feminine adornment reflected the Third Order regulations of her century. St. Joan's utterly spiritual and utterly secular lives became a single involvement with God and man that should typify tertiary life in the world.

Someone has said that God writes straight with crooked lines. Perhaps it was partly a matter of political expediency that brought the Third Order into eminence very quickly. Cardinal Hugolino, later Gregory IX, wished the tertiaries to take vows in order that they might be exempt from military service, which the medieval serf owed to his lord. Thus the anti-papal Ghibellines would lose an important source of military personnel. Naturally, then, the Third Order was not popular with feudal masters, but its cause was espoused by popes and bishops. The situation of the members was akin to that of the conscientious objectors of subsequent centuries who protested wars they deemed unjustified.

The Third Order is not, therefore, to be just another parish or inter-parish society. It does not merely touch one part of a Catholic's life nor simply add an extra chore; it is a new way of life. But evidence of the *public profession* of the Gospel must be restored to tertiaries. They have their habit, but it is not visible in modern life. They have a fraternal community, but its apostolate is not very often the compelling example of the Christ-life that it ought to be. A Rule, Constitutions, novitiate, profession, and visitation give them a canonical structure. Their office and spiritual conferences give them a liturgical community. Yet their charism as a group is not always evident to the Church and to the world. It is easy enough to say that the testimony of a good life is enough identification. But insofar as Franciscans are given by God for the salvation of the world, tertiaries must demonstrate the Gospel in lay life more visibly and not just as an appendage or mere lay affiliate of the First Order. This latter viewpoint is reinforced in the minds of Franciscan priests by the very brevity of the "course" in Third Order direction given them, like an afterthought, in their seminary days. (We had best omit reference to instruction about forming Franciscan women religious.)

The Third Order laymen—who once pronounced religious vows—are an important, even an essential part of the total Franciscan charism, since the Apostolic Age obviously consisted more of lay persons than priests and consecrated women. First Order priests are chaplains and creators of liturgical community, but members of the fraternity themselves should propose, decide, and lead the group according to their inspirations. The chaplain (who can be a diocesan priest) is the liaison with the hierarchy, which preserves the orthodoxy and mission of the Church. He is the spiritual adviser of *collegia poenitentium*, or "gatherings of penitents," as tertiaries were sometimes called. Besides presiding over the liturgical community, which is the source and root of the social-action community (*Decree on the Ministry and Life of Priests*), the chaplain counsels the individuals to the measure of their existing potential to apply the Gospel to their careers, family lives, budgets, and apostolate. He visits the homes of the ailing members and those who live too far away to attend the meetings. He avoids so overwhelming them with his personality and directives that the members are too paralyzed to act out their own insights. He gives them the attitude of *continentium*, another word used by St. Francis. It can be translated "abstainers," "self-disciplined," or "those who withhold themselves" from the world while not rejecting the world.

Chapter IX

FRANCISCAN PRAYER LIFE

CHRIST IS PRESENT whenever two or more are gathered in his name, whether at prayer or in other godly actions, including eating, studying, recreation. But he is preeminently present in the commemorative sacrifice and meal. All forms of common prayer should bear a close relationship to this eminent presence of Christ in the Eucharist. Actually one should not make a radical cleavage between "official" and "non-official," because God's family is in action in either case. Liturgy has a broad meaning; its first translation is "the public business," or "the community in action." The praise of God and thanksgiving thus remain the first order of business, in which the presence of Christ can have several dimensions.

Because the presence of Christ is more obvious and effective in the liturgy, the *praying community* initiates the spiritual bond between men. It gives energy and formulation to the Christian *social* community, which is the face-to-face group of household, parish, or friary with which one has stable contact. Out of it evolves the *serving community*. Concisely stated, after their encounter with God at worship, wherein the members gratefully consecrate the bread and wine, they turn to each other and to the world, wherein they gratefully consecrate man's secular activities. "Gratitude" is one translation of *Eucharistia*. They remember that it was at the Last Supper that Jesus remarked, "I am in your midst as the one who serves you" (Luke 22:27), and that he washed his Apostles' feet.

He prays well during the liturgy who shares in the *action* of the congregation. This is the "horizontal" approach to God, of which we hear so much. The worshipers enter the procession, sing, rise, and respond. They reflect upon and try to share in the sentiments being proclaimed in the rite. But this is generally nonemotional; hence it leaves some worshipers unsatisfied, accustomed as they may be to more affectivity in prayers. Nevertheless, even though these liturgical actions are official and do not rise spontaneously from the worshiper's emotional investment, one supposes that they demonstrate and provide for joy, love, enthusiasm, gratitude, sorrow, filial fear. The silences during the liturgy give some opportunity for communing with God informally and for deeper emotional involvment. This is the "vertical" prayer, made individually to God, which is the norm of private prayer and reflection away from the group. Vertical prayer has a stronger emotional tone, because one discusses with God such matters as career, family, the future, personal sinfulness, specific anxieties.

We remember that St. Francis called himself a "poor little worm" in one of the prayers attributed to him. Although this phrase very nearly echoes David's psalm[1] describing the sufferings of the virtuous man and also prophesying the role of the Messiah, in itself such a passage is inadequate as a phrase in common prayer, because the participants cannot be sincere without some feeling of self-depreciation at a given moment. Each worshiper must accurately discern, in private communion with God, what best expresses his passing need. This distinction seems essential in drawing up the ceremonials and books of prayers for a religious institute. Otherwise the merely personal and transitory prayers of religious founders are thrust upon generations of followers.

---

[1] Cf. Psalm 22, verse 7.

Incidentally, with respect to "poor little worm," as a *continuing* self-concept, it would be suspect in any prayer.

All prayer should be geared to action or change, whether in the individual's behavior or in the community's service. This is analogous in the personal life of any religious with his vow of celibate chastity. The person is freed to love God without distraction—but that is insufficient. The celibate, man or woman, is wedded to the Church just as Christ is wedded to the Church. The virgin can love all the individuals of the community equally and intensively in his or her love of God. The daily renewal of this particular vow is a prayer that leads to social action.

Contemporary liturgical reformers remind us to make all forms of prayer, especially group prayer, conform with the varying seasonal Eucharistic liturgy—whence the development of Bible vigils, the administration of sacraments during Mass, and the paraliturgies, or prayer practices associated with the liturgy. St. Francis, like most men of faith, accurately saw the Eucharist as the focus of Catholic life. He revered priests, including unworthy ones, precisely because they consecrated and administered the Body of Christ. From his deathbed he wrote letters to the minister general and to the whole world about the reverence due to the Blessed Sacrament. He makes a similar reference in his final *Testament.* Early in his religious life he chose France as his preaching territory (1217) because of the respect for the Eucharist there. He frequently directed his brothers to sweep out and adorn churches as the true house of God. He was accustomed along the road to turn toward the nearest tabernacle when he was unable to reach a church for the time of prayer. At Greccio, the scene of the first Christmas crib, he placed a host on an altar stone that was set in the crib—as a kind of paraliturgy. Similarly, as he lay dying at the Portiuncula, he blessed and broke bread for the brothers who attended him.

The viability of any liturgical community depends on a reasonably small size—perhaps no more than thirty—which generally obtains in religious houses or the Third Order fraternity. Larger communities should break up often into smaller groups based on mutual ties of age, apostolate, and the like. Spontaneous prayer life is more comfortable in such a setting. According to the limits of their apostolates, First Order priests should build up community by concelebration; at least one evening a week should be sacrosanct for concelebration of Mass and the sharing of dinner and recreation. Although community spirit is primarily an attitude, it does not long survive without concrete expression. Religious Brothers and Sisters of our orders, who do not *form* communities of Christians, as do the priests by their ministry, should nevertheless *build up* the community of their apostolate— students, neighbors, the sick, their spiritual clients. (This was emphasized in the chapter on community life, pp. 60-71; it is reiterated here as a part of Franciscan prayer life.)

Our members should be as free as St. Francis to express themselves in contemporary forms of liturgy—the dialogue homilies, spontaneous Collects, and petitions in the Prayer of the Faithful. In group meditations no one should be forced to contribute; then again, no one ought to be fearful of offering an insight or conviction. In paraliturgies, such as the Chapter of Faults, members can take the occasion to apologize for unkindnesses. To expose one's emotional life is the keenest risk a person can take, for he does not have weapons with which he can defend himself, as in physical or intellectual risks. Perhaps it is better to chance the occasional excesses of some persons rather than stifle self-expression in the cause of that sobriety which is just this side of indifference. In all these matters of "experiment" and "transparency," a person must be judged in the context of his whole spiritual life insofar as it is apparent—zeal for souls, kindliness to others, theological orthodoxy, faithfulness to the Franciscan charism. If an individual finds little good in existing prayer forms, if he feeds his ego by being *avant-garde*, if he surrounds himself with a "fan club," one has reason also to doubt his genuine transparency.

The prayer life of an institute should express its charism and not be a mere aggregation of the personal whims of past and present superiors. Reducing the number of prayers is not the whole point, either. Ceremonies of investiture, profession, renewal of vows, traditional paraliturgies, and so forth reinforce an order's self-concept or existential personality. Franciscan prayer life should revolve about the concepts of being "minors," of reliving the Apostolic Age, of the humanity of Christ, of local apostolates, of freedom of self-expression, of optimism about man's perfectibility, of joy in the created world, of poverty, of true secularity, and of serving the disadvantaged. Our three orders need to develop these concepts even in the Mass by the choice of readings. They should seek permission to substitute such Franciscan elements as a Preface based on the *Canticle of Brother Sun* and a Canon using parts of St. Francis' paraphrase of the Our Father, or the long prayer in Chapter Twenty-three of the *First Rule*. The liturgical greeting could be "The Lord give you peace," which our founder says was directly revealed to him by God. The final benediction might be the blessing of St. Francis to Brother Leo, which is the prayer of the high priest in the Pentateuch (Num. 6:24ff.).

It was mentioned earlier in this chapter that sentiment—not sentimentality—is crucial in Franciscan prayer life. Our men have traditionally been popular preachers with a simple, down-to-earth style; thus their ministry has been informed by their prayer life. The best way to be sure of one's hierarchy of values is not by an intellectual process, but by discerning the matters about which one feels strongly. One can apply this norm to prayer also. Whom do you love? What do you fear? Where do you find joy? How is your enthusiasm kindled? What goals give you satisfaction? Which accomplishments have brought you most peace and inner repose? Prayers which never have the support of an emotion (apart from the obvious fact that many persons do not easily verbalize or demonstrate emotions *externally*) may not touch the areas of one's sincere values, but only those which we think we ought to have, because they have been imposed by the order, by society, or by the exigencies of an apostolate to which we are not fully committed. Secular tertiaries must understand this, too.

Any comments about Franciscan prayer life would be incomplete without mentioning its simplicity. Except for the days of retreat and the novitiate, our prayer life eschews introspection and self-analysis which bespeak an overemphasis on the ego. We do not classify ourselves in the illuminative way, the seventh interior castle, or the twelfth rung of the ladder. We gravitate to simple ejaculatory prayer and the prayer of quiet gaze or self-disciplined contemplation, for which all forms of prayer are a preparation.

"My mind is so filled with Scriptural passages," St. Francis claimed, "that it has enough for prayer and reflection. I do not need anything beyond what I know about the poor crucified Christ" (Celano, *Second Life*). His *Rule* prescribed a shorter form of the Divine Office than that used by the monks; unlettered brothers were to recite Our Fathers. Beyond this and the Mass, each brother was left to the inspiration of God. The breviary and Mass provided spiritual reading; meditation needed no prescribed hours. At that time this was true of the monastic orders as well. In subsequent centuries, when the nature as well as the language of liturgical prayer was slowly forgotten by the majority, priests and lay people multiplied popular devotions in order to feel some contact with God and his saints. How useful and relevant these are to modern Franciscans must be assessed by the individual. Thus the Way of the Cross with formulary prayers might be useful for a group from time to time, but private reflection at the Stations appears to be a better meditation.

One biographer tells of the simplicity of St. Francis' prayer life. He could apparently pass a whole night with the aspiration

"My God and my all!" Although Christian prayer life *begins* with immersion in the humanity of Christ as the means of knowing the Father, it does not necessarily end in Christ. The Son sends some rare persons forward for brief encounters with their heavenly Father. They must surrender their anthropomorphisms in order to enter the black emptiness of the indescribable God. At such times the human imagination has no proper object, and the humanity of Christ does not mediate the direct encounter with God. The inner mystery of the Divine Persons touches a man at this point; and it is the Word, rather than the Word-made-flesh, with whom the human person must identify to become a son of the heavenly Father. At such a moment the life of God is not in a man so much as the man is in the life of God. Of course, one must continually return to the Word-made-flesh as the support and center of the spiritual life processes, because mystical moments pass quickly in the workaday world. In our Seraphic Father we see the ultimate of both forms of prayer: the stigmata, from identification with Christ; and the ecstasy of direct, wordless contact with the Father, who cannot be apprehended by any categories of the senses.

Chapter X

THE RATIONALE OF ASCETICISM AND JOY

MORTIFICATION is irrevocably bound up with the religious state in the eyes of most persons. Some religious assume that a rather consistent crossing of nature is a kind of price God exacts for grace. It is as if one should feel guilty in religious life for enjoying anything too much. Books of customs for some institutes warn against such diverse "wickedness" as stroking a cat or celebrating a birthday—because it hearkens back to the days when we were "in the world." In the attempt to become detached from the beautiful and refined, some religious became attached instead to the ugly and, worse, to a smug self-concept of "holier-than-thou." A great deal of such mortification, unrelated to practical ministry, does more to destroy the psychic energy necessary for human growth than to retard the sin which is corrosive to human growth. The seven deadly sins derive from the same basic drives as creativity, play, rest, awareness of one's perfectibility, the imitation of ideal figures, physical fitness, and so forth.

Nevertheless, it seems spiritually dangerous to dismiss offhandedly what apparently nourished the mystical life of the Church for so many centuries. The first Eastern monks were hostile to the senses as if it were a terrible onus to have a body—which is not very sound theology. St. Benedict, on the other hand, prescribed a life style not unlike that of the Italian peasants as to food, garb, and rest. St. Francis, however, merely repeated the ascetical directives of the New Testament, which are usually very general applications of "the cross." The only concrete injunction he added was prescribed fasting in imitation of the Lord. The restrictions in garb merely echoed the Lord's command to his Apostles about a second tunic. The Third Order *Rule,* which St. Francis did not himself write, required the same modesty in dress and social functions, but with more abstinence than the Church at large practiced. But even from this, members were excused if pregnant or traveling, and during bloodletting, and on holidays. When St. Francis heard at a Chapter that many brothers used hair shirts and metal devices to inflict pain on their bodies, he *forbade* these outright. Perhaps he feared that pride might result, or that physically exhausted brothers would be useless in the ministry, or that there was some psychological danger in keeping the physical aspect of human existence so continually before the mind.

There was some development here in St. Francis' thought as he clarified his charism and related his life style to the Gospel directives. In the *First Rule* he wrote, "The Spirit of the Lord wishes the flesh to be mortified and despised, and to be held of little value, lowly, and contemptible" (Chapter Seventeen). In Chapter Ten of the same *Rule* he tells the sick to thank God, "for those predestined to eternal life are mortified by rods of suffering, weakness, and a spirit of sorrow, as the Lord remarks, 'Whoever is dear to me I reprove and chastise' " (Revelation 3:19). Yet St. Francis was equally solicitous in his *Rules* for the alleviation of the suffering of the ailing brothers. If the "flesh" merely represented what was hostile to the Spirit of God, even in this passage one would have no quarrel with the founder. In any case, the *Second Rule,* which actually contains more concrete directives than the prior writing, does not make such statements about the vileness of the body.

If the Franciscan mandate is to reduplicate the Gospel life, one must turn to the pages of Scripture to see how the Apostolic Age remembered the life of Christ and transmitted its impressions to subsequent centuries. Jesus gave no ascetical prescriptions outside the context of making the life of preaching and service more effective—no staff for the journey, taking up one's cross daily, giving one's goods to the poor so as to be free of encumbrances on a tour of duty. Prescinding from what St. Francis thought was useful asceticism for his personal spiritual growth, we see that he legislated and taught and permitted only what served the brothers' ministry. The apostolic life was the rationale of asceticism. In his backward look at his life, the *Testament*, Francis observed that he began to do penance and that what was bitter to nature became sweet on the occasion of his first *ministerial* act, which was in imitation of Christ's frequent service— that is, St. Francis began to nurse the lepers and even to kiss their limbs. Asceticism grows out of ministry, rather than the reverse—which latter frankly appears to be the slant of religious formation all too often; that is, if you keep stifling the demands of nature by an active program of physical and mental denial, God will favor the assignment you are given. This is the "savings-account" mentality—so much grace for so much mortification. Sin is a "debit" and fasting pays a "dividend."

In St. Francis' view, the mere absence of deliberate sin and the self-control of mortification are pseudo-perfection. Misery is fruitless and asceticism is pointless except as a share in the mystery of Christ—that is, not so much the Christ of the Passion, as the Christ struggling with anxiety and tension from establishing his messianic position and extending God's kingdom all during his earthly sojourn. This is the ultimate, ministerial meaning of the tribute paid by St. Francis to the asceticism of Brother Ass before his death. "I give testimony that it has been in every way obedient, refusing nothing, but anxious to fulfill every command; Brother Ass neither avoided exhaustion nor escaped discomfort in order to achieve my demands" (Celano, *Second Life*).

In a sense it is not enough to probe only the New Testament in order to clarify the rationale of Franciscan asceticism. As a lawgiver Christ was the second Moses, and as a voice of God, the last of the prophets. In himself he summed up the destiny of God's family; he relived its crucial moments of history. Like Moses, he spent forty days alone with God; like Israel, he wandered in the desert of temptation. In each instance God had to sustain and provide even the nourishment to keep his people alive and trusting in his fatherliness. Austerity was not so much chosen as imposed by the exigency of establishing God's kingdom in the Old and New Testaments. The anguish of Israel over Egyptian fleshpots and the temptation of Christ to yield to mere nature are a kind of suffering inescapably related to the extension of God's kingdom. Men are incapable of spiritual success until they depend on God. Israel must be chastised through human agents, as during the Exile, in the sense that self-dependence automatically removed Israel from God's care. Just as St. Paul was later to remark about God's choice of the foolish and weak, Zephaniah spoke of the "remnant" of the spiritually hungry and apparently powerless Israelites who were to continue God's family (cf. Zeph. 3:12-13). They were the *anawim*, the poor in spirit.[1]

Poverty of spirit in the religious institute or in lay life is more related to asceticism than to material poverty as we usually apply that first beatitude. Another translation of *anaw* is "meek"; so it is used to describe Moses in Chapter Twelve of Numbers as the meekest man on earth—one who was so unprepossessing that Aaron had to speak for him, yet a man utterly dependent on God in his personal anguish of soul. Mary, God's lowly and obscure handmaid, remarked in her Magnificat that God struck

---

[1] I am indebted in this section of the chapter to the writings of Barnabas M. Ahern, C. P., particularly *New Horizons* (Notre Dame, Indiana: Fides, 1965).

down the proud and mighty in the conceit of their hearts, while he tenderly looked after the cause of his *anawim*. Similarly St. Paul gloried in his weakness because the power of God thus became more obvious.

Suffering in its own right, therefore, originally had no meaning in Jewish and Christian thought. It cannot be isolated from the context of God's family being built up and finally perfected at the end of the world. So Isaiah, speaking in the person of Yahweh, tells Israel to keep a better fast and to do more appropriate penance than that of sackcloth and ashes to win his favor. Rather should they forgo false claims, ease each others' burdens, and share their homes, clothes, and food with the needy (cf. Isa. 58:4-9). Christ preached and practiced this kind of "penance" as a dimension of his apostolate also. Hence the risen Lord told his disciples on the way to Emmaus, "Did not the Messiah have to undergo all this so as to enter into his glory? (Luke 24:26)" The suffering of Christ culminated in crucifixion, but it was always present in his anxiety to fulfill his mission by preaching and in his compassion for those *anawim* whom he served. He himself was the supreme *anaw*, for in his ministry he had less than the foxes and birds; he had not whereon to lay his head. It was not merely the cross of Calvary that he carried; he denied himself and took up the cross of ministry daily. Asceticism in this case is not predicated on the depravity of man, but on his perfectibility and potential spiritual dignity. When Christ tells his disappointed Apostles, weary of an unsuccessful ministry, that some devils are cast out only by prayer with fasting, the matter is best understood as deprivation of rest, of visible success, and of feelings of satisfaction and exhilaration. The Apostles are to go off alone to pray and fast in order to become *anawim*; they are men bereft of human consolation and fanfare, dependent on God alone to nourish them, isolated in their hearts, and deprived of human power in their ministry.

In both his *Rules*, therefore, St. Francis links fasting and that spirit of prayer to which all human endeavors must cede. He captures the mind of Christ in the *First Rule*, Chapter One, when he quotes Matthew 19:21 and 16:24; and Luke 14:26. Like the Master himself, our founder delineates his charism by telling us that asceticism is a consequence of the Gospel life more than a prior requisite. Three principles suggest themselves from the foregoing concepts. (1) The servant of Christ must reckon with the hostility of "the flesh"—which in St. Paul's writings means the burden of Adam's sinfulness, or the difficulty of responding to God's message of love. Such obstacles in himself and his clients lead the Christian to depend on God alone for effectiveness. (2) Those who aspire to the Franciscan charism, including secular tertiaries, must forgo physical comforts, spiritual consolation, human fellowship, and so on, in a kind of self-denial appropriate to their state in life. (3) The degree of their dedicated love of God's family is assessed by their availability to those who need the word preached to them, and their accessibility to those who require healing, leadership, teaching, counseling, prayers, or whatever else the servant of God is able to provide.

Religious poverty is one expression of this asceticism. One must "risk" living by God's providence without storing up wealth and investments. If God inspires a new apostolate, he will provide the means; that is one way of determining whether a work is divine or merely human in origin. Another expression of this asceticism is celibacy, which frees the religious to love God's whole family. Virginity considered only as physical integrity in a man or woman is too narrow a definition. The celibate becomes an *anaw*, risking emotional desolation and hunger for acceptance of his ministry. The married Franciscan tertiary who understands his charism must take the same risks of not acquiring status symbols (poverty) and of losing the affection of his family (an extension of celibacy) in his exhorting others to do good (preaching) and in his hurrying to the aid of the disadvantaged (service).

In this sense St. Francis made the religious or evangelical life common property of even the married.

It is even more important today than in St. Francis' time that we serve as a beacon of hope to man in his "existential frustration," as the saying goes. We must "suffer with," or have compassion. Sociology today tries to engineer human destiny. Studies and statistics are destroying man's individuality and creating some faceless "norm" or "median" as the typical standard around which we all gravitate. Behavioral sciences dictate the acceptable personality factors that often place the greatest stress on the very persons least able to acquire those factors. Therefore it seems that we are needed now more than ever before.

St. Francis himself did not set up standards of acceptability. In his *First Rule* he said that even thieves are to be received in the friary. He must have remembered the occasion when he was driven away from a monastery because of his tattered appearance. Another time he changed the way of life of some brigands whom he served with courtesy and respect; a few of these men later entered the order. St. Francis realized that hunger often reduced men to robbery in those hard days. He could call anyone "brother" and mean it, whether the person appeared evil, was rejected by others, or lacked the graces prized by worldlings.

This availability is learned in religious life (of all three Franciscan Orders) by bearing with the irritations and invasions of privacy within one's own religious family. This is not to say that putting up with drafts, leftover food, and headaches has no value—it has, particularly because these are mortifications of the passing moment, not chosen by ourselves. But the greatest value of these discomforts is to support and prepare the way for apostolic mortifications at the hands of rude or intrusive persons whose demands are unforeseen by us. In our own religious or blood-related families it is a ministerial act to listen to endless accounts of others' migraines, to lend a typewriter or umbrella when we are about to use it, or to accept the unsought advice of a would-be therapist. Just as the best training in sociology is to live among those with social problems, so the most important ministry to God's family is to one's own immediate family.

The title of this chapter links asceticism to joy. One's apostolate as a Franciscan must be casual and relaxed, since it ultimately depends on God for success. It must not be cluttered by too many rules of approach beyond kindly humor and brotherhood with fellow sinners. Struggle must coexist with laughter, and serious effort with being amused by one's own limitations. It is true that many individual acts of religious life must be performed with grim determination, or out of justice more than spontaneous charity. Acceptability to God does not depend on joy. But when joy is habitually absent, there is a real "credibility gap" for oneself as well as for the world regarding the value of this vocation.

No one skips through life with a perpetual smile of joy; no one's heart is light when he gets out of bed onto a cold floor early on a winter morning. But St. Francis reproved the dour visage and melancholy attitude. Only sin should make a brother sad. He called his brothers God's minstrels and *joculatores*, or "jokers." He even legislated joy in Chapter Seven of the *First Rule:* "The brothers should show themselves joyful and content in the Lord, merry, and becomingly courteous."

Joy is a part of that optimism which tells a man he will win the next race or the one after that. So at our profession ceremonies we are not covered by black palls prostrate on the floor with a funereal tolling of bells to announce our death to the world. Conscious, rather, of the total Paschal mystery, including the resurrection, we sing *Te Deum*, congratulate one another with a kiss of peace, sing our snappiest hymns. Then, delighted that we have been given to the world for its joyful salvation, we have a great party afterwards.

Chapter XI

FRANCISCAN POVERTY

THERE IS A TENDENCY for religious of our time to isolate certain factors in the life of poverty and make these factors the total definition of poverty. This vow is now variously called one of "detachment," of "economy," of "dependence," or of "permission." It may be that such a factor is the totality of poverty for some religious institutes, especially if their life style depends on large holdings of land or expanding investments; each institute must clarify its own charism. In any case, detachment and permission do not excuse one from asking himself whether the possession or project being sought at a particular moment is really compatible with one's type of poverty in the first place.

Nevertheless, all the factors named above are typical of any poor person who has little of his own. Once more, however, in the case of religious the absence of individual ownership could still allow considerable ease, even indulgence, under collective ownership. Each institute's charism, however, must serve to make Christ present to the Church and to the world, and every true gift of the Spirit must build up and receive the approval of the body politic. In the spirit of continuing reformation, meaningless types of poverty must cede to the significant. The previous chapter already proposed the principle that the vow of poverty is primarily a type of *asceticism that is consequent upon the ministry* of preaching and service—at least in our three orders. Further, the factors of secularity and mobility condition the life style of a Franciscan. It may be useful, therefore, before specifically treating St. Francis' legislation and exhortation, to consider some general notions of poverty as understood by the Catholic and non-Catholic world, to whom we are sent as a sign of the Apostolic Age come alive.

We may well wonder, if we ever achieve the "great society" without poverty, whether in such an environment we as religious can live in relevance without possessions. (What would some religious do nowadays without an "inner city"?) Would such a nation or world look upon us as anything but relics of the past, were we to live, cashless and comfortless, in this theoretical land where there was abundance for all? Would we have to redefine "poor" people merely as those lacking in spiritual wealth? Analogously, if teaching, healing, and other institutional services became so technical and diversified that the religious institute could not provide adequate training any more, would the service aspect of Christian ministry fall into desuetude?

Apart from this "paradise" existing only in the speculative imagination at present, other expressions of poverty (and service) would evolve, we can be sure, from reflection on the Gospel, just as modern social principles have been drawn by Christian thinkers from the pages of Scripture. The personality of an order, as it was defined earlier, bespeaks potentials not yet arrived at. At all times the Gospel life of an available and mobile ministry would be the criterion of poverty. This refers not so much to what you *use*, but rather to how much you allow yourself to *be used*. Those whom we serve are more interested in the "psychological" austerity and self-denial mentioned in the last chapter than in the lack of material appurtenances in life. Once more, we not only serve God's *anawim*, but must become *anawim* ourselves in the sense that we *accept the conditions and clientele of the ministry* that God provides, rather than set up somewhat arbitrary levels of possession and use of material goods as absolute norms. We remember that that Man who had not whereon to lay his head during his mission frequently stayed with Lazarus, Mary, and Martha and enjoyed the refinements of an apparently wealthy home. And one can be sure that Mary, the mother of Jesus, as well as other friends, provided what comforts they could while the Lord was on the road. All this is written not to disparage traditional religious poverty, but to put it into proper context. Christ—and here is the point—was as satisfied with poor as with comfortable accommodations. In the very important enumeration of the beatitudes, the lowly, miserable, and deprived—the *anawim* —are identified more by spiritual than by material factors.

The best testimonial to poverty in an institute would be the coexistence—without jealousy or complaint—of many levels of poverty according to the kinds of ministry. If optimism and freedom of expression are a genuine legacy of St. Francis, this should be possible. In any case it is dangerous to establish uniform regulations for "possession and use"; it is a fetish of a falsely democratic society. If a certain amount of "cash and comfort" becomes an inalienable right, members develop an attitude that they should by all means use up all they are entitled to. They soon forget that they become *anawim* by reducing their needs.

Poverty has always been such a characteristic of the order that some Franciscans would make it the primary mark of our life. As a matter of fact, centuries ago Pope John XXII declared it a theological error that evangelical poverty was the highest form of imitation of Christ. Love of our heavenly Father, charity for our neighbor, apostolic availability, obedience to any life style the Spirit designs for us—such virtues supersede poverty in living the Christ-life. Just as it is false spirituality to assume that the vow of celibacy denigrates sex or human passion or the body of man, it is equally out of step with the Scripture to conclude that the material advantages of this earth are evil. Hence poverty is not the same as tasteless living quarters, clothes, and food. Beauty and practicality are more Christian than their opposites. Whatever threatens the mental well-being of the apostle

or disciple of Christ with respect to possessing either too much
or too little is the wrong kind of poverty for him. One's ego is
so involved—and properly so—with satisfaction in his ministry,
that each person must consider himself in the double role of
a Christ-figure and a professional person. The individual conscience is the final forum: like Christ, the Franciscan must be
uncluttered by the *impedimenta* of living; as a professional, he
must use the secular world's techniques. We read nowhere in the
New Testament that Christ deliberately imposed any form of
poverty on himself outside the context of the ministry. Some
exegetes think that he even belonged to the middle rather than the
lower class of Jews. He once rebuked Judas' false concern for the
poor by remarking that they are always with us and lauding
the use of a valuable perfume on his body. He told no one merely
to dispossess himself, but to give one's possessions away as a part
of entering the ministry alongside him. Dispossession forced a
person to become *anaw*, that is, dependent on God and inspired
benefactors for support.

It is specious, therefore, to reason that large and efficient
plants, such as hospitals, printeries, or schools, make witness to
poverty impossible. In some cases, because of government sub-
sidy or required standards of excellence, large operations are
necessary. In this case, poverty consists of serving a poorer
clientele and of expecting a modest fee—or none, if this can
possibly be arranged. It is likewise specious to compare the social
service of religious with the Peace Corps or governmental agencies.
(We can readily see that the motivation of the latter is typically
as noble as that of religious.) But social servants, after all, are
paid. Volunteers, as in the Peace Corps, return to their past
life and to freedom. It is unfortunate that members of religious
orders prize themselves and their spiritual orientation so little.

When we work with and for the poor and disadvantaged, it is
true that we may give better witness by identification with them
in their physical environment. But unless we share our facilities

and talents and resources, we have merely descended to their level without helping them to rise to a higher level. There seems to have been a time in history when sharing the life style of the poor was a very persuasive testimony to the following of Christ; this may have been predicated on the assumption that people could not move very easily anyway from one social or economic class to another. In modern times we see a great fluidity of wealth and of the levels of society. Therefore, the poor are not automatically impressed simply because we share their lot. They want to be shown how to rise to a higher standard of living. For example, a missionary in South America, while presenting himself as willing to live in the milieu of a back-country farmer, must assist his people to arrive at a higher standard of living by improved techniques and contacts with the twentieth century—whether it be a matter of credit unions or brick-making. The missionary to the poor, recognizing human value, exposes the poor to a better life. In the process he hopes that the poor will have more time for study, will achieve leisure, and will investigate the meaning of life through religion. In other words, where religious once taught implicitly through poverty that it was virtuous to share the lot of the suffering Christ when it was inescapable, now they are called upon to emphasize that it is not virtuous to be disadvantaged if it is possible to escape the situation. This is, once more, the service-aspect of their total ministry. The nineteenth-century Franciscan missions of California are a parade example. The apostolic life of poverty must be interpreted differently according to local needs of the apostolate. The general Constitutions of an institute must be broad enough to provide such flexibility.

In the progressive countries where advanced technology is a substantial factor in the way of life, religious are called upon to demonstrate that the modern life can be more than crassly materialistic. The humanistic psychologists point out the opposition between Technology and Eros—that is, between the

inexorable machine and the liberating power of human love-rela-
tionships. An outstanding example of the real compatibility of
the two in a context of poverty was the saintly Franciscan and
martyr of charity Maximilian M. Kolbe. He was optimistic, for
he accomplished his life's work with less than one lung. He
made himself accessible to the spiritual needs of his time by
printing a daily newspaper and many periodicals in his native
Poland. He was mobile enough to establish a similar, flourishing
foundation in Japan. He was innovative in using airplanes to
make deliveries and in planning to make popular movies and set
up television broadcasts as early as 1939, when war broke out in
Europe. He creatively allowed his *several hundred* friars at
Niepokalanow to develop patents and to build the largest and
most efficient printing plant in Central Europe. Yet the personal
poverty of the friars there is still a legend.

In Chapter Two of the *First Rule* St. Francis seems to set a
general norm of his order's poverty: "The brothers are free to
receive anything that the poor are accustomed to have, with the
exception of money." Chapter Fifteen forbids the brothers to
ride horseback or to have a beast of burden, because poor folk
generally did not. It would have been incongruous for a brother
to arrive on horseback in the morning and ask a farmer to work
in his fields for payment in produce or ask a weaver for a bolt
of cloth at the end of the day. Candidates had to dispossess
themselves; if that was impossible because of prior commitments,
their good will sufficed. In the *First Rule*, unlike the *Second*, the
founder permitted money for the care of the sick friars and lepers
(Chapter Eight). St. Francis probably had no other apostolates
that required ready cash at the time he wrote the *First Rule;* there
were neither houses of formation nor seminaries for clerical
candidates. But the principle is nevertheless established by this
provision and another directive of the *First Rule* which was applicable to lay-brother candidates and then extended to priest
members; that is, they were to possess the tools necessary to the

trade they practiced upon entering—utensils, instruments, pots, or whatever. Since the Gospel points out that Christ had a treasurer among the Twelve, St. Francis' attitude is at first difficult to grasp. Perhaps he saw that money was the chief symbol of the competitive and materialistic middle class just beginning to emerge in the thirteenth century. He himself knew how it had enabled him to lead a life of selfish indulgence as a youth. He likewise saw that the financial security and storehouses of the existing monasteries kept the monks from living in contact with other men and earning their keep along with and by means of preaching God's word and serving others.

Only if their labor did not support them were the brothers to beg alms. Before the Pope, Francis compared himself to a poor woman who had borne many sons to the king of the land; since they bore a family resemblance to the king, they were—without being embarrassed about it—to ask him to support them. The implication of the story is apparent. But the friars' own labor was to be the chief source of their livelihood. St. Francis learned this after Bernard of Quintavalle and Peter Cataneo, wealthy men, dispossessed themselves, joined St. Francis, and set about collecting alms to live on. The people of Assisi grumbled about the "parasites" whose help to the poor was transitory and merely created a couple more beggars to support. Thus, as sociologists put it, their "role opposites" helped the first Franciscans to define their relationship with society. In any case, the brothers were to continue with these principles: live in the style of poor people; not to store up provisions beyond the present necessity; share what resources they had with the poor; support themselves by their own labor rather than beg; live austerely precisely because imitation of the itinerant Christ necessitated freedom from possessions.

St. Francis said he would gladly strip the altar of the Virgin Mary to give to those really in need; her Son would send someone to restore to his mother what she had lent to the poor. Yet he did not look down upon and judge the rich; they were to help support good persons who were living the ascetical life of service. In nothing were the brothers to judge others, especially the wealthy (*Second Rule*, Chapter Two). Above all, if they did have to beg, they were to demonstrate the spirit of joy in privation. St. Francis seemed to have a particular block about money as such, but he did not hesitate to receive all of Monte Alverno as an outright gift from Count Orlando Chiusi. Once more, personal experiences conditioned a founder to incorporate certain points into the *Rule*. It almost seems a fixation with St. Francis: "If we should happen to find money anywhere, let us not consider it more than dirt under our feet. . . . Should any brother collect or possess money or coin [except for the necessities of the sick, as was mentioned], all the rest should consider him a false brother, a thief, and a robber—the owner of a purse— unless he were really to have a change of heart" (*First Rule*, Chapter Eight). Nevertheless the general attitude of the saint on poverty is insightful and is magnificently recorded by his biographer: "To the degree that the brothers neglect poverty, the world will neglect them. They will seek, but not find. But if they lean on our Lady Poverty, the world will support them, precisely because they have been given to the world for its salvation" (Celano, *Second Life*).

Chapter XII

LAW AND OBEDIENCE

OBEDIENCE is the most difficult vow to understand and practice in an age of democracy and personalism. This vow must also be seen in the light of the Franciscan charism, particularly its self-expression and mobility. Another factor in this charism, optimism about man's perfectibility and good will, should characterize superiors in their trust of the subject's convictions and insights.

The presence of a superior should bring one greater security that he is being loyal to and sharing in the mission of the Church, rather than inflating his ego. Praise and acknowledgment—those very important functions of a superior—serve to reinforce the subject's zeal and to buffer his frustrations. Some contemporary authors reject the word "subject" in religious life—for one is subject only to God. Rather, they say, one should refer to "co-workers." Whereas this has considerable merit in view of St. Paul's mention of his own "co-workers" in the Church, "subject" puts a religious in the mind of Christ—the supreme identification in the life of a Christian: Christ was subject to Mary and Joseph in all things, subject to Jewish rituals during his ministry in Palestine, and subject unto death under Roman law.

When we read of the Church in the Acts and the Epistles, we do not see authoritarianism, however. Peter himself served and in a sense obeyed the mandates of the believing community, particularly the voice of the Apostolic College. In Chapter Eight of the Acts, we read that it was they who sent Peter and John to lay hands on the Christians of Samaria in order that the latter might receive the Spirit. We do not read much about the assertions of authority in the Apostolic Age. The numbers of Christians were few enough to be like a family or fraternity. Since they commonly held that the return of Christ was imminent, there did not seem to be much purpose in a "staff and line" organization anyway. Meanwhile, whoever had most closely witnessed the significant acts and words of the Master automatically enjoyed the greatest influence. From this we can at least glean a concept that a superior rises to leadership from knowing the mind of Christ, rather than being adept in sensitivity sessions or knowledgeable in the apostolic techniques of the local community. One hopes, of course, that a superior knows both Christ and the skills of the twentieth century.

Psychologists state that an important task in the maturation process is an increasing tolerance of reasonable frustration. Setting aside the problem of those neurotics who become superiors at times (because they actively seek office or have it thrust upon them), some subjects are simply unable to tolerate reasonable frustration, perhaps because of childhood experiences or a lack of the spirit of the *anawim*. They should recognize themselves as unsuited to religious life, especially if they find themselves hostile to a superior who gives evidence of zeal and optimism himself. It is just that not everyone has received the gift to obey. We easily grant that not every superior has the ability to clarify his thinking to his subjects. St. Teresa of Avila once remarked that she would prefer a learned to a pious spiritual director (she was not speaking of a superior in this case), if she could not have both. Notwithstanding her preference, most subjects would be reassured if they knew that the superior habitually listened to God during prayer as his primary obligation to his subjects. We remember that the theological and canonical experts advised the Pope not to approve St. Francis' charism at the outset. Assuming now that God intended the work of the saint to flourish, we read that only one Cardinal came forward to support the movement; he said refusal would be tantamount to saying that the Gospel is an impossible ideal.

Let us examine the words and actions of St. Francis himself and set them in the context of the life the first followers actually lived. At first glance it seems as if he legislated the kind of obedience that contemporary authors are disparaging. As we examine his words and acts, it is necessary to distinguish the statements of a perfected and heroic soul about his personal virtue from the actual legislation for the imperfect and typical person who enters religious life as a "school for perfection." St. Francis commands us by his legislation; he draws us by his example. Every person decides for himself what the basis for his obedience will finally be.

It was written of Francis that he made a corpse-like obedience his own option. He once said that he would even let wild beasts devour him without struggling, because their strength and ferocity were given to them by the Lord. To the extent that denial of one's instinct for self-preservation is irrational (since there is no motive here of dying for another), one cannot make it part of the Franciscan charism. To the degree that such statements symbolize subjection to the *known* will of God, no one would oppose them. We have to recognize and contend with many dramatic remarks of St. Francis. "Do not mention impossibilities. Were I to command anything beyond your natural strength, then obedience would become strong enough for it" (Celano, *First Life*). Though a superior who conducts himself according to this principle may note with satisfaction that the subject was, indeed, able to be pushed a little further, one would hope that he is also able to see whether he is pushing his subject closer to a mental and spiritual breakdown.

Elsewhere St. Francis asserts that he would obey a novice of an hour's standing as quickly as a wise and experienced brother, since "the less important the one who governs, the greater the subjection of the one governed" (Celano, *Second Life*). Although one is tempted to think that no one would presume to command the founder during his lifetime, as a matter of fact, when the provincials demanded a written constitutional form of government rather than a day-to-day commentary by him, St. Francis dramatically resigned his patriarchal authority and promised obedience to Peter Cataneo, his vicar. He asked the latter to place a superior over him, moreover, so that he would continue to grow in grace. Further, acceding to the voices of the elected ministers and at the behest of his friend Cardinal Hugolino, he wrote the *First Rule* of twenty-three chapters—despite his lifelong discomfort with written documents and what he feared might be rationalizations about the Gospel life. Even so, despite his protestations of subjection, in the incontrovertible words of his later *Second Rule* of 1223 he still considered himself the supreme arbiter of the Franciscan Order: "The brothers are obliged to obey Brother Francis and his canonically elected successors" (Chapter One). It seems, therefore, that St. Francis never intended to alter his role as mentor of the order, but was willing to live in subjection with respect to his daily conduct, for he says in his final *Testament*, "I wish to be a prisoner in the guardian's keep, so that I may not take a step or perform an action outside obedience and his desires, for he is my lord."

Apart from the personal life of the founder, we can learn much about the life style and obedience of the first friars. In the same document, the *Testament*, St. Francis writes, "All the brothers are obliged to obey their guardians." Apparently not all the friaries had such a superior, because further on he directs the brothers to report any lapses of faith or liturgy to the *nearest* guardians. In the *Second Rule* he also distinguishes between a *house* and a *place*. We must keep in mind the astounding liberty of the first decades of the First Order—greater than religious ever enjoyed before or after in any of the major foundations in the history of the Church. The brothers were almost entirely "laics" at first, not "clerics." Like the *braceros* of the United States,

they went off for the day or for many days to earn some payment (in the friars' case, it was payment in kind, not in money).
In this way the brothers supported themselves and the poor.
Because they "free-lanced" continually, they were not bound to
seek constant permissions, make many reports, or follow a con-
ventual routine—until the priestly and monachizing element
prevailed in the order. This fluid life style was possible only when
the friars were neither tied to cultic and sacramental ministrations
as priests, nor bound to regulated institutional life as teachers or
nurses. In any case, St. Francis would consider it incredibly
complicated to expect subjects to wear a path to the superior's
door as most existing Constitutions require. He gives general
directives about obedience in the *First Rule*. The brothers should
gladly serve and obey *each other* in the spirit of charity. (This
is analogous with fraternal correction, which is not left to superiors alone.) The professed, he writes, should not wander about,
beyond the pale of obedience. This seems to refer to the daily
manual labor mentioned above.

In fact, the founder always seemed more preoccupied with the
functions and personality of the superiors rather than with those
of the subjects. In Chapter Four of the *First Rule*, Francis concerns himself with the role of the minister as being more crucial
than that of a guardian. The ministers are to visit the brothers
often, admonish and console them, and remember that the Savior
came to serve, not to be served. They are to give good example,
lest they have to answer for the loss of any brothers on judgment
day. In Chapter Five of the same *Rule*, St. Francis uses the
hendiadys "ministers and servants" seven times to reinforce the
concept of service. Nowadays we read a great deal about *diakonia*
as the primary dimension of authority in the Apostolic Age. The
other dimensions are *marturia*, the witnessing to Christ's life by
the testimony of his saving action in oneself, and *koinonia*, the
fellowship of community action. These three components of
authority in the early Church, when set alongside St. Francis'

life and writings, reinforce the validity of the assertion that his charism was to restore the Apostolic Age to the Church. Perhaps nowhere does this attitude come through more clearly than in St. Francis' description of an ideal minister general in the *Second Life* by Celano. He is to be a man without inordinate attachments, fond of prayer, and responsive to individual needs without favoritism. He should project the image of simplicity rather than learning. He ought not to be fixated on hobbies or collections, lest this distract him from his office, which is a burden more than an honor. Fully available to others, he must console the afflicted, being their ultimate fraternal comfort. Otherwise, with no place left for them to go for healing, the disease of despair will undo them. In order to teach meekness to the high-spirited, he has to lower himself and not thrust his authority upon them. Finally, he must demonstrate the tenderest pity to the lost sheep who have deserted the order, because the temptations that would drive a man to such desolation must be overwhelming, indeed.

As in the primitive Church, a lay order, such as St. Francis originally had in mind, needed little display of jurisdiction. When pulpit-preaching and sacramental administration became extensive activities of the order, St. Francis incorporated directives into the *Second Rule* about clerics' activities in relationship to bishops. Already when St. Francis wrote to St. Anthony in Sicily about teaching the brothers theology, the number of clerics in the order was growing; here was the beginning of our seminaries of theology. At the Chapter convoked on May 23, 1260, when the Constitutions of Narbonne were being compiled from all the earlier decrees and interpretations since the time of the founder, St. Bonaventure forbade the admission of "lay brothers" into the order, except when domestic chores required it—and then they were to be admitted only with the permission of the minister general. Other prescriptions were written into the general law that St. Francis may have wondered about. Despite his wanting even the walls to be rubbed with meat at Christmas, the eating of meat was never allowed inside the friary—a monastic practice. The young friars were ordered to confess twice weekly and receive Holy Communion at least fifteen times a year—which in those days would be considered very frequent reception. The friars also had to have a companion when they left the friary. Finally, the voluntary fast after Epiphany mentioned by St. Francis in the *Rule* was made mandatory thereafter.

We realize in retrospect that St. Bonaventure had to contend with separatist, even heretical elements in the order. But whether all of his measures and inhibitions clarified or obscured the mind of the founder must be judged likewise in retrospect. When the Cardinal Protector of the Poor Clares, Giovanni Gaetano Orsini, who was later to be elected Pope Nicholas III, asked St. Bonaventure to take back jurisdiction over the Second Order, the latter insisted that the Clares maintain a strict enclosure and that they have the support of endowments and funds without depending on their neighbors' largesse. Neither was according to the mind of St. Francis and St. Clare, who were very relaxed in their personal relationship. On her deathbed Clare was at pains to secure the Pope's written confirmation of her "privilege of poverty." The point of this digression in a chapter on obedience and laws is that, while the existential personality of an order does imply evolution, the multiplication of laws by authority, especially if the body politic is not consulted, is likely to impede, rather than facilitate the expression of a charism. For this reason, during the post-Vatican-Council renewal of religious life, legislation is the last, not the first act of a General Chapter. Our understanding of the mechanics of government, such as length of term of office and the manner of election, is much less important than understanding the balance between *institutional* and *charismatic* elements of religious life. Wherever there is no clear command in canon law, on the one hand, or in a founder's description of his charism, on the other, considerable discretionary powers should be left to the local superior—or, rather, the subject himself. This is merely an intelligent application of the principle of *subsidiarity*.

In order for law to be most effective in *freeing* people to serve God, those who live under it should have an extensive voice in its formulation, so that it is already an "internalized" conviction. Law is a coin with two faces. One side is changeless: the nature of man's psychological makeup, the authority of God over man, the example of Christ as the supreme "law of the Gospel," and especially the charism of the institute. A candidate to the order or a member knows that these elements are not contestable. The reverse side of the coin has changeable elements, but the value remains the same, even though the mint mark and date give us added information about the time and place from which the coin came. Constitutions and interpretations are similar to the changing inscription of the coin. This side of the "coin of law" represents the expectations and self-understanding of the membership in differing ages and circumstances. These expectations become the Constitutions that keep the charism alive; they are not an inviolable "sacred cow." St. Francis himself had a problem with this; he did not at first want "glosses" on the *Rule*, which is the nature of Constitutions. He heard that some superiors were interpreting his *Rule* quite flexibly, and so he gave general permission to the *entire* order to disobey whatever was not "to the letter." Cardinal Hugolino saved the day by countermanding St. Francis, who obeyed without question.

In this last matter St. Francis shows considerable ambivalence. In his final *Testament* he forbade glosses on the *Rule*, yet from about 1212, when annual Chapters became typical, he framed many statutes to interpret his charism. This was even prior to the General Chapters that began five or six years later. The whole process, according to the *Legend of the Three Companions*, consisted in collecting Gospel quotations with a brief exegesis. They say that he tried many rules before he wrote one down. Among the *Opuscula* edited by the Quaracchi Franciscans, there is a letter to a minister general, possibly Brother Elias, written by the founder. St. Francis interprets some points of his *Rule* and asserts, "For these and whatever other points in the *Rule* that are not so clearly stated, you will with God's help provide fulfillment." When some personal or apostolic need arises, St. Francis gives his followers full freedom. "In a moment of obvious necessity the brothers should act as the Lord inspires, for necessity has no law" (*First Rule*, Chapter Nine).

The provincial or local superior should ask his subjects as a group to establish their self-expectations and their expectations of each other. Once this is clarified, his obligation is to see to it that these expectations are met. Thus any individual opposition represents alienation from the community, rather than a private conflict with the authority. Further, this enables the superior to become the focus of the community's apostolate and social life. He gives the means to an apostolic end, once he understands the subjects' purpose, without having to seek permission from higher superiors. The immediate superior merely asks to be informed of the subject's needs and progress for two reasons. If he is successful, the subject can be praised and reinforced. If unsuccessful, the subject can be buffered, his feelings protected, the pieces picked up for a fresh start—and the superior can take some of the blame emanating from higher authority, since we assume that he has greater interior resources and graces in his post.

The superior forbids and prohibits whatever imperils the personality and life style of the order with one hand, and releases the spiritual energy of his subjects with the other. Personal freedom does not confer the liberty to *thwart* the law, since even on a local level the members have formulated the law, but it constrains one to *act out* the convictions by which he has freely bound himself. The difficulty is to locate and train superiors who would be of this mind. St. Francis realized this. In Chapter Eight of the *Second Rule* he provided for the deposition of a minister who was a poor servant of the brotherhood. And when a subject felt that he couldn't observe the *Rule* conscientiously under some local conditions, he was to have recourse to the minister, who is ordered to apply the "golden rule." In this passage St. Francis does not seem to believe in so-called "blind obedience." He remembers the attitude of Christ, who called his followers "friends," no longer "servants," because the Holy Spirit would soon descend to give an understandable rationale to "everything I have commanded you" [to observe]. In both his *Rules* St. Francis is careful to exempt a subject from a command contrary to conscience. The implication is that one might have to obey God against the superior. But one must be willing to take the consequences, even as Christ did before the Sanhedrin and Pilate. Whereas one is released from obedience to a superior, one is not free from paying the price, while maintaining interior and exterior peace for the good of the order. A Franciscan who would rather remain in the order within a situation of persecution and frustration, especially if he is sincerely trying to follow his conscience and be loyal to the charism of St. Francis, will be blessed by the saint in time and eternity.

The ultimate truth each religious experiences for himself is this: a man can be free every day of his life even if he decides every day of his life to be bound by another's will.